Roman History

A Captivating Guide to Ancient Rome, Including the Roman Republic, the Roman Empire and the Byzantium

© Copyright 2018

All rights Reserved. No part of this book may be reproduced in any form without permission in writing from the author. Reviewers may quote brief passages in reviews.

Disclaimer: No part of this publication may be reproduced or transmitted in any form or by any means, mechanical or electronic, including photocopying or recording, or by any information storage and retrieval system, or transmitted by email without permission in writing from the publisher.

While all attempts have been made to verify the information provided in this publication, neither the author nor the publisher assumes any responsibility for errors, omissions or contrary interpretations of the subject matter herein.

This book is for entertainment purposes only. The views expressed are those of the author alone, and should not be taken as expert instruction or commands. The reader is responsible for his or her own actions.

Adherence to all applicable laws and regulations, including international, federal, state and local laws governing professional licensing, business practices, advertising and all other aspects of doing business in the US, Canada, UK or any other jurisdiction is the sole responsibility of the purchaser or reader.

Neither the author nor the publisher assumes any responsibility or liability whatsoever on the behalf of the purchaser or reader of these materials. Any perceived slight of any individual or organization is purely unintentional.

Free Bonus from Captivating History (Available for a Limited time)

Hi History Lovers!

Now you have a chance to join our exclusive history list so you can get your first history ebook for free as well as discounts and a potential to get more history books for free! Simply visit the link below to join.

Captivatinghistory.com/ebook

Also, make sure to follow us on Facebook, Twitter and Youtube by searching for Captivating History.

Table of Contents

PART 1: THE ROMAN REPUBLIC 1

   INTRODUCTION – THE ROMAN REPUBLIC: AN EMPIRE BEFORE THE EMPIRE..........................2

   CHAPTER 1 – THE PAST THAT MADE IT POSSIBLE: THE FOUNDATION OF ROME BETWEEN MYTH AND HISTORY 5

   CHAPTER 2 – DOWN WITH THE KINGS: THE PAST THAT MADE IT HAPPEN 9

   CHAPTER 3 – EARLY REPUBLIC 13

   CHAPTER 4 – MILITARY ACHIEVEMENTS OF EARLY REPUBLIC: TAKING ITALY 20

   CHAPTER 5 – MIDDLE REPUBLIC: THE PUNIC WARS AND MEDITERRANEAN DOMINANCE...............24

   CHAPTER 6 – THE MILITARY VS. CULTURAL DOMINANCE: THE ROMAN CIVILIZATION MEETS THE GREEK WORLD 32

   CHAPTER 7 – LIMITLESS POWER AND THE BEGINNING OF THE END: THE LATE REPUBLIC 37

   CHAPTER 8 – THE AGE OF THE GENERALS: POMPEIUS, CRASSUS, AND CAESAR..................42

   CHAPTER 9 – SENATUS POPULUS-QUE ROMANUS (SPQR) AND ITS DOWNFALL 45

   CHAPTER 10 – THE RISE AND FALL OF JULIUS CAESAR AND THE END OF THE ROMAN REPUBLIC 48

- CONCLUSION.. 54
- TIMELINE... 56

PART 2: THE ROMAN EMPIRE 59
- INTRODUCTION 60
- CHAPTER 1 - FROM THE REPUBLIC TO THE EMPIRE: THE RISE OF OCTAVIAN 62
- CHAPTER 2 - THE AGE OF AUGUSTUS 69
- CHAPTER 3 - THE JULIO-CLAUDIAN DYNASTY AFTER AUGUSTUS: FROM TIBERIUS TO NERO 75
- CHAPTER 4 - CIVIL WAR AND THE YEAR OF THE FOUR EMPERORS (AD 68-69) 85
- CHAPTER 5 - THE FLAVIANS 88
- CHAPTER 6 - THE NERVA-ANTONINE DYNASTY: THE FIVE GOOD EMPERORS (AND A COUPLE OF NOT SO GOOD ONES) 93
- CHAPTER 7 - SOME NEW EMPERORS 103
- CHAPTER 8 - CRISES, CIVIL WARS, AND DIVISIONS: THE LONG AND PAINFUL DECLINE 107
- CHAPTER 9 - TWO EMPIRES: EAST AND WEST 110
- CONCLUSION 113
- TIMELINE OF IMPORTANT EVENTS 114

PART 3: THE BYZANTINE EMPIRE 119
- INTRODUCTION 120
- CHAPTER 1 - LAYING THE FOUNDATION FOR THE BYZANTINE EMPIRE 123
- CHAPTER 2 - THE AGE OF CONSTANTINE 127
- CHAPTER 3 - FROM CONSTANTINE'S DEATH TO THE FALL OF THE WESTERN EMPIRE 131
- CHAPTER 4 - THE AGE OF JUSTINIAN, THE GREATEST RULER OF THE BYZANTINE EMPIRE 138
- CHAPTER 5 - HERACLIUS 144
- CHAPTER 6 - THE ICONOCLASTS: LEO III THE ISAURIAN AND CONSTANTINE V 147
- CHAPTER 7 - THE COLDBLOODED EMPRESS IRENE OF ATHENS 150
- CHAPTER 8 - TINY STEPS FORWARD: THEOPHILUS AND MICHAEL THE DRUNKARD ... 153
- CHAPTER 9 - A NEW GOLDEN AGE: BASIL THE MACEDONIAN AND HIS DYNASTY 155
- CHAPTER 10 - THE CHANGE IN THE HOUSE OF MACEDON: NICEPHORUS PHOCAS AND HIS NEPHEW 161
- CHAPTER 11 - BASIL II THE BULGAR SLAYER 165
- CHAPTER 12 - ALEXIUS COMNENUS 167

CHAPTER 13 – THE COLLAPSE AND FALL OF THE EASTERN ROMAN EMPIRE 170
CONCLUSION 176
THE TIMELINE OF THE BYZANTINE EMPERORS 177
HERE'S ANOTHER BOOK BY CAPTIVATING HISTORY THAT YOU MIGHT LIKE 182
FREE BONUS FROM CAPTIVATING HISTORY (AVAILABLE FOR A LIMITED TIME) 183
REFERENCES 184

Part 1: The Roman Republic

A Captivating Guide to the Rise and Fall of the Roman Republic, SPQR and Roman Politicians Such as Julius Caesar and Cicero

Introduction – The Roman Republic: An Empire before the Empire

When we think of ancient Rome, the first notion that comes to mind is the one of the empire, followed by the image of a mighty emperor, his legions, colossal buildings, and the Gladiators (or the rhetoric and poetry, depending on your preferences). Some may recall the image of a "unified" Europe under a single sovereign – the emperor of Rome. However, Rome did not become remarkable at this considerably late phase. In fact, many historians see the history of Rome under the Emperors as a long, gradual decline. Centuries behind, many Romans shared this view. They talked and wrote about their glorious past obsessively – but who wouldn't? Their past made the empire not only possible; it made it real. It was during the Republic that Rome gained an empire. Most of the achievements that the first emperor of Rome, Octavian Augustus, claimed to have completed were, in fact, earned during the Roman Republic.[1]

Why is the Roman Republic that important?

The Roman Republic shaped the unique culture of Greco-Roman fusion as we know it from art, literature, rhetoric, philosophy, architecture, and law. The rise of the Republic was the rise of the city of Rome – once a small, ordinary Italian settlement that had become a metropolis with a million inhabitants who dominated the Mediterranean. The notion of Rome's republican politics influenced great minds from Plutarch, Tacitus, and Shakespeare, to the philosophers of the European Enlightenment, and the American Founding Fathers. It is still relevant today. Another fusion - the one of the classic republican political system and the culture of spectacle and performance - still defines our world at every possible level. The image of Roman legions served as a basis for the clone and Stormtrooper legions of the fictitious Galactic Empire. The assassination of Julius Caesar, on the other hand, has given the pattern and excuse for the killing of tyrants in the real world, ever since.[2]

The history of ancient Rome is the history of western civilization and a significant part of the history of the world. The Roman culture is the foundation of our own culture and politics. Our ideas of liberty and citizenship, as well as the terminology of modern politics, including senators and dictators, have been defined and thoroughly used in antiquity. The way we laugh at ourselves and the world around us, too. The world's finest satire-writers were ancient Romans. They invented entertainment through fear as well. Even though the Romans did not write horror novels (if they did, those novels would undoubtedly be amazing just as their works in other forms), they watched horror in the arena. The outcomes of their bloody spectacles with the Gladiators were unpredictable. But let's not go too far. In this book, we'll have a close look at the beginning of Roman civilization, the foundation of the city and the Senate, the expansion of the Roman Republic, its glory, and its end.

The Republic of Plato or...

You'll recognize many elements of present-day democracy, including its ugly side, blatant political marketing, reputation management, populism, intrigue, and the occasional murder. Indeed, the Romans used to kill each other way too often for such civilized folks, but they justified those assassinations eloquently and convincingly. Thanks to the abundance of written documents from the Romans themselves, we can delve deeply into their motives and ambitions, and discover the real stories behind most controversial events that involved treasons, spy-mistresses, and murders.

The Roman Republic had two faces. One of them was impeccably clean, with white togas,[3] high rhetoric, the advanced constitution of the city-state, and an elevated sense of virtue, justice, and pride. The other face was characterized by the lust for power, conspiracies, and obscure wealthy individuals who ruled from the shadow, letting others do the politics in public. Some Roman politicians loved to say they were living in the ideal state - the Republic of Plato, while in fact, Rome was instead the *faex* (feces) of Romulus, as Cicero joked in a private letter.[4]

The culture of ancient, republican Rome was one of openness and diversity from the very beginning. The sense of identity and belonging was based on the idea of citizenship, not the origin. Highly educated people discussed the nature of freedom and the problems of sex, just as we do today. But this cosmopolitan city also had a dark side. The glorious political constitution turned out to be rotten inside. There were also slavery, filth, and illnesses everywhere. Death was just around the corner on the streets, just as it was in the Senate. Eventually, the Roman Republic fell entirely by itself.

The end of the Roman Republic was also a new beginning, as it resulted in the foundation of a new era known as the Roman Empire. This will be the subject of the book two in this series.

Chronology

You can find a precise timeline at the end of the book. For now, let's just sketch the history of the Roman Republic in a few short sentences. The mythical city foundation took place in 753 BC. The authentic Roman republican political system was developed by the late fourth century BC. The third century was a period of bloodshed, struggle, and uncertainty, marked by the Punic Wars. The second century was an antithesis to the third; Rome's legions almost effortlessly defeated Hellenistic towns and kingdoms throughout the Mediterranean. Rome had become huge and immensely powerful. And corrupt, soon after. The first century BC is one of the most exciting periods in world history and, especially, in the history of Ancient Rome. New turmoil was caused from inside. Political fights, corruption, lawlessness, and civil war characterized this period. Few generals controlled the political scene and held all the power, while the traditional institutions became useless. That was the age of Cicero and Catiline, Julius Caesar and, at the very end, the Emperor Octavian Augustus, with whom this period (and this book) ends and the next begins.

Chapter 1 – The Past that Made It Possible: The Foundation of Rome between Myth and History

This history of the Roman Republic begins with a mythical tale. The Emperor Octavian Augustus had employed various notable cultural workers, the most important of which was certainly Virgil, who wrote an account of Troyan hero Aeneas, depicting him as the founder of Rome. Augustus needed to create a new national myth and establish a different—nicer and cleaner—sort of cultural identity. However, the first, authentic story the ancient Romans could resonate with was the one that follows.

There are a couple of good reasons, to begin with, the story of Romulus and Remus. Firstly, the Romans themselves included the tale in their histories. They did not do so because they were naïve. They were, in fact, just as skeptical about the notion of a wolf feeding two human infants as we are. They told the story over and over because it was important. It shed - and it still does - a special light to the very sense of Romanness. It tells a lot about whom the Romans were and how they saw themselves. Another reason is that, simply, we've got no choice. We've got no proof the story is either false or true. Any archeological evidence had been eaten up back in antiquity, thanks to a constant, intense process of urbanization.

Finally, in a broader sense of the term, history does include the knowledge of myths and legends. Surprisingly, it looks like the Romans did not think much about the origin of the world, as their central myth is not about the creation of the Universe (aside from the tendency to make Rome the center of it) but of the foundation of the city. Therefore, we'll take a closer look at this fascinating story.

A Tale of Rape, Murder, and Abduction – the Legend of Romulus and the Foundation of Rome

Myths are weird. A commonsense logic doesn't help to process them. All myths have strange and illogical elements, but this one is particularly bizarre. The story of Rome is full of unheroic elements – let's add throwing newborn babies to the list in the heading. Its protagonists belong to the lowermost level of society, and include murderers, possibly prostitutes (Livy[5] points out to the similarity between the word wolf and a colloquial expression used for a prostitute, and wonders whether it was the former who took and breastfeed the baby brothers), outlaws and runaways from all around the peninsula and beyond.

There are many different versions of the story, and a couple of them had been written down in ancient times. While Cicero avoided writing about supernatural elements (he only mentioned the odd detail of the god Mars as the father of the twins, and moved on, focused on geographical assets of the place Romulus had chosen for the city). Other writers, such as Ovid, made fun criticizing the way Romulus solved the problem of establishing the first Roman marriages and families. The most detailed account of Romulus's life and the early history of Rome – and the one we will stick with – is the one of Livy.

Act One: Divine Rape and Failed Infanticide

So, this is the story. Once upon the time, there was a little kingdom called Alba Longa. Its king, Numitor, was thrown out from the throne by his brother, Amulius. To make sure there would be no throne pretenders from his brother's line, Amulius forced Numitor's daughter, Rhea Silvia, to become a virgin priestess. However, she was not quite a virgin; soon it became clear she was pregnant. Now, there are two explanations for her pregnancy. Rhea Silvia claimed the god Mars raped her. Many ancient writers believed the claim and wrote about a *disembodied phallus coming from the flames of the sacred fire.*[6] Livy, on the other hand, was thinking what we are thinking. The god of war was just a convenient invention to conceal an entirely human affair. Anyway, the priestess gave birth to two boys, and Amulius quickly ordered his men to throw the newborns into the river Tiber to drown. The servants could not bring themselves to complete the task, so they left the babies on the shore. A *lupa* (either a female wolf or, as Livy assumed, a prostitute) found them and offered them her nurturing breasts. Finally, a compassionate shepherd took them in.

The Capitoline She-Wolf was an icon of Rome since antiquity. The age and origin of the figures is a subject of controversy. The *Lupa* was long thought to be an Etruscan work of the 5th century BC, with the twins added in the late 15th century AD, but radiocarbon and thermoluminescence dating has found that it was possibly manufactured in the 13th century AD.
Rosemania, CC BY 2.0 <https://creativecommons.org/licenses/by/2.0>, via Wikimedia Commons
https://commons.wikimedia.org/wiki/File:She-wolf_of_Rome.JPG

Act Two: Family Reunion and Fratricide

When they grew up, the legendary brothers accidentally met their grandfather Numitor, helped him to reclaim the throne of Alba Longa, and left to establish their own city. Unfortunately, they could not agree on the precise location where they should find the city. Out of the famous seven hills, Romulus picked the Palatine, whereas Remus opted for Aventine. Romulus paid no attention to his brother's wishes and started constructing the defenses around his preferred site. Remus insultingly jumped over them, and Romulus killed him, shouting afterward: "So perish anyone else who shall leap over my walls."[7]

Act Three: The Asylum

The city had been built with Romulus as the sole ruler. There was just one problem left – Rome had very few citizens. Romulus came up with an innovative idea and declared Rome an asylum. He encouraged the outcasts of the rest of Italy to join him. The city was soon filled with convicted criminals, runaway slaves, and other immigrants. But there were no women, and without women, there was no future. Romulus made a new cunning plan. He invited the neighboring peoples to a festival. The Sabines and the Latines, whole families, came in great numbers. In the middle of the proceedings, Romulus signaled his men to capture the young women among the guests and to take them away as their wives. There is no consensus over how many accidental brides were kidnaped (the estimates vary from 30 to 683), yet the very first Roman marriages started off with mass abduction and rape.

A Poetry Interlude

"O Romulus, you are the only one who has ever known how to reward his soldiers;

for such pay, I would willingly enroll myself beneath your banners."

—Ovid, *Ars Amatoria*[8]

While "serious" Roman thinkers, such as Cicero, Livy and Sallust tried their best to either justify or condemn Romulus's decisions, less serious ones were openly ironical. The poet Publius Ovidius Naso – widely known in our century as Ovid, the author of *Metamorphoses* – included the famous legend in his most controversial work, *Ars Amatoria* (*The Art of Love*). Ovid refers to the rape of Sabine women to point out that the theatre has always been a good place to meet girls. It was Romulus who "first mingled the cares of love with public games." We'll never know for sure whether those (and many similar) lines compelled Augustus to banish the poet from Rome, or the *Ars Amatoria* was just an excuse for the expulsion, hiding some political secret. Augustus certainly had a lot to hide, and Ovid's links with the emperor's grandchildren made the poet very unfortunate. His exile has been revoked in AD 2017.[9] We can certainly agree it was slightly too late.

Epilogue

The captured Sabine women – now wives and mothers – bravely stopped the war that was initiated after their abduction. According to the legend, the young wives entered the battlefield and begged both sides – their Sabine fathers and Roman husbands – to stop fighting. They did not want to become orphans or widows, and they said they would rather die themselves. Their mediation worked and resulted in peace. Rome became a shared Roman-Sabine town, under the joint rule of Romulus and Titus Tatius, the Sabine king. Tatius was murdered a couple of years later, the same way as many other Roman rulers and politicians were yet to die: violently, during a riot. The pattern of fratricide and civil conflict was established early in the Roman history.

Chapter 2 – Down with the Kings: The Past that Made It Happen

According to Livy, Rome had been under the rule of 'kings' – seven of them – for two and a half centuries. Romulus disappeared mysteriously during a storm. Either he had ascended to the heavens as the god Quirinus[10], or this was another political murder, yet a primitive monarchy had already been established.

We are still somewhere between myth and history. The primary sources for this period are part fables – part historiography, but they are still very important for the history of Rome. Many details about the kings do not make much sense. Their chronology is most obviously problematic; seven kings over the 250 years would mean each of them ruled for more than three decades, on average. That consistent level of longevity is physically impossible. More probably, either the monarchy lasted much shorter than the Romans estimated, or there were more kings in between.

The first of the six kings following Romulus was a Sabine called Numa Pompilius. He was said to be an easygoing individual who conceived most of Roman religious traditions, including the Vestal Virgins, the title of Pontifex, and even the modern western calendar with all its months. The second monarch (or third if we count from Romulus) was Tullus Hostilius, a notorious warrior responsible for the demolishing of Alba Longa, the ancestral city of many Romans. Next was Ancus Marcius, Numa's grandson. He was both a warrior and a tradition keeper, and the founder of the Rivermouth, Rome's seaport at Ostia. The fourth king after Romulus was Tarquinius Priscus, also known as 'Tarquin the Elder.' Unlike his predecessors on the throne, he was of the Etruscan origin. He expanded the city, established the Roman Forum and the Circus Games, and initiated the work on the great Temple of Jupiter on the Capitol above the Forum. His successor Servius Tullius was a political reformer who devised the Roman census and defined the city by the construction of the Servian Wall.

A Patricide: The Death of Servius Tullius, the Last Honorable King of Rome

Servius Tullius deserves our special attention, for several reasons. He was "the wisest, most fortunate and best of all Rome's kings."[11] Yet he was the only king whose father's name had been omitted from the list in the Forum. Roman kings had diverse backgrounds: Numa and Titus Tatius were Sabines; Tarquin the Elder came from Etruria and had a Greek (Corinthian) origin. Servius Tullius's case was special. According to the ancient legend, Servius had no father; his mother (who was a servant; hence "Servius") was said to have encountered and was penetrated by a divine, fire-made phallus.[12] He was in fact either the son of a slave or a war prisoner. His case is yet another example that even at the very beginning of the Roman political order, 'Romans' could come from somewhere else. Even those born very low (including ex-slaves and their sons) were allowed a chance to rise to the top.

And there is more. Servius Tullius was the first to arrange a census of the Roman citizens, officially registering them in the citizen body and categorizing them in different positions matching their wealth. He used this census for organizing the Roman army and the voting and elections system. The army was organized in 193 'centuries,' characterized by the sort of equipment the soldiers used. The equipment was linked to the census category. It was supposed that the richer the soldier was, the more massive and valuable equipment he could provide for himself. Eighty centuries of men were classified from the richest, in a full kit of heavy bronze armor; to the fifth class that was equipped with just slings and stones.

According to Livy, the Roman Republic was mostly founded on the efforts and achievements of Servius Tullius. But Livy had something more interesting to tell about, and this was the most controversial part of the story. Servius Tullius had two daughters, and both were called Tullia - Tullia the Elder (Major) and Tullia the Younger (Minor). He wanted them to marry the sons of Tarquin, the Elder, and so they did. But Tullia the Younger and Lucius Tarquinius (married to Tullia, the Elder) arranged the murders of their siblings, then married and plotted the assassination of Servius Tullius. Coldblooded Tullia encouraged her husband to convince senators secretly, and he went to the senate-house followed by a group of armed men. Lucius Tarquinius gathered the senators and gave a speech condemning Servius, pointing out that ultimately he was a slave born of a slave. He said Servius had failed to be selected by the Senate and throughout an interregnum, which was the tradition for the election of kings of Rome, and was, instead, gifted the throne by a woman. Moreover, Tarquin criticized Tullius for supporting the lower classes over the wealthy. Tullius indeed took large parts of the land of the upper classes and distributed it to the poor. Tarquin was not happy about instituting the census either, as it exposed the affluent upper classes to lower classes' envy.

The king came to the senate-house determined to defend his position, but he had no opportunity to speak. Tarquinius threw him down the steps and ordered his men to murder Servius in the street. As if it was not enough, Tullia came with her chariot and drove over her father's body. Tarquinius even refused to allow Tullius's burial, which earned him the nickname "Arrogant" or "Proud" (Superbus).

Tullia Minor Drives over the Corpse of her Father[13]
https://commons.wikimedia.org/wiki/File:Bardin_Tullia.jpg

The Arrogant King and the Death of Roman Monarchy

The last Roman king was the son of Tarquinius Priscus, Lucius Tarquinius Superbus, known as 'Tarquin the Proud'- a distrustful tyrant who mercilessly liquidated his opponents. He was married to Servius' daughter, but he overthrew him and grabbed all power. He ruled by fear, ignoring the Senate, which had already been established and had the function of advising the king.

Tarquin the Proud (or Tarquin the Arrogant) selfishly exploited the Roman people and forced them to work on his building projects. The behavior of this king and his family eventually led to public revolt. The breaking point was another rape – one of king's sons, Sextus Tarquinius, raped the virtuous Lucretia. The innocent victim killed herself with a knife, and the revolution had begun, which brought the end of monarchy and the establishment of the 'free Republic of Rome' in late sixth century BC.

The man who drew forth the knife that stabbed Lucretia's heart was Lucius Junius Brutus, the ancestor of a more famous Brutus – the conspirator against Julius Caesar. Brutus gathered the Roman people and banished Tarquin and his family. In 510 BC, the Roman monarchy was over. Two elected consuls replaced the king at the top of society, and the Roman Republic was founded. The first two consuls were Collatinus, the widower of the unfortunate Lucretia (and formerly a close friend to Tarquin's sons), and Brutus.

The Romans vs. the Kings

Ancient Romans had a somewhat problematic relationship with their history, especially with their kings. Tarquinius Superbus was widely loathed and, after his spectacular fall, kings became an object of hatred. There was nothing more dangerous politically than to be accused of wanting to be called a king. Even the emperors were highly cautious and would never tolerate being called a king. But Roman writers saw this issue slightly differently. They recognized the regal period as the source of their major religious and political institutions. Romulus founded the city, and other kings developed it. Even though they were later despised, kings were recognized as the creators of Rome. This was sometimes exaggerated. Rome's ancient historians tended to depict the regal period as more modern and its achievements as more grandiose than they were or even could be.

Chapter 3 – Early Republic

The Dawn of Liberty

Contemporaries and many ancient historians celebrated the end of the monarchy as the birth of freedom as well as of the free Roman Republic. The city of Rome had a fresh start – as a 'public thing' (*res publica*). A new form of government was established. Brutus and Collatinus (the latter was unfortunately exiled shortly after because of his family links; he was, in fact, another Tarquin, and his full name was Lucius Tarquinius Collatinus) became the first consuls of Rome. Consuls were the central public officials of the Republic, in charge of many aspects that used to be the duties of the king. They managed the city politics and were military generals. In a way, their role was very similar to the one of a king and their power was sometimes seen as a 'monarchical' quality in the Roman political system. Their emblems and symbols of the office looked very much like those of their kingly predecessors. But there was a considerable difference between the two political regimes. Consuls were chosen entirely by the vote of the people of Rome, and they could hold the function for only a single year at a time. One of their responsibilities was to preside over the election of their successors. Finally, the power of consuls was both limited and temporary; it was always shared between two consuls and lasted up to a year.

It remains unclear though how and when exactly did the *res publica* begin. Livy and other ancient historians presented a clear narrative of what was most likely to be chaos. Were Brutus and Collatinus the first consuls or were they just said to be so by much later Romans? Most probably, the latter was the case. Ancient writers loved to imagine their traditional institutions went back much further than they did.[14] Contrary to the much-celebrated tradition, the new order and the entirely different form of government could not be established instantly. It was a slow, gradual and messy process that lasted for centuries. Rome's representative institutions took shape at some point between 500 BC (the end of the Tarquins) and 300 BC (the time of Scipio 'Long-Beard'). During this period, the Romans slowly defined the underlying principles of Republican politics and civil liberties. They formulated 'what it was to be Roman' and their 'way of doing things' that characterized their subsequent imperial expansion. The most important element that distinguished Rome from every other classical city-state was their idea of citizenship, civil rights, and responsibilities, which still survives in our times. Somewhere during these two centuries, Rome finally began to look 'Roman.'[15]

The Clash that Defined Rome: The Conflict of Orders and the Twelve Tables

So, what happened during those two hundred years? The fifth and fourth centuries BC were full of internal and external conflicts and tensions. The internal politics of the early Roman Republic are characterized by a dispute between the patricians and the plebeians. The modern term for this clash is the 'Conflict of the Orders.' The old story goes as it follows. After the expulsion of Tarquinius Superbus, the power fell into the hands of a group of aristocratic families collectively known as the patricians.[16] Only members of these families could hold religious and political office. They were the ones who elected (among themselves) two annual magistrates called 'consuls' and sometimes during crisis selected a dictator to take sole charge of military matters. Then, at some point between 494 and 287, patrician power and supremacy were challenged by plebeian protest.[17]

The antagonism between the patricians and the plebeians was not simply the antipathy between the rich and the poor. The plebeians were not just Rome's poor. All Roman citizens who were not the members of any of the very few patrician families (such as Claudii, Julii, and Cornelii) were categorized as plebeians. Some of them were wealthy, and they were not very happy to accept that they didn't participate in governmental structures. They required an equal share of political power. Even though they could not use the existing political system (which was entirely controlled by the patricians), they had the support of most of the Roman people.

The poorer Romans struggled to maintain their farms during their military service. Some of them turned to patricians for help and fell into debt. That way, they became vulnerable and open to abuse by their creditors. Poor people were becoming slaves to patricians, and their position became unsustainable. In 494 BC the plebeians revolted against the patrician treatment of those among them who fell into debt.[18] So they decided to go on strike. When the consuls ordered out the army in 494 BC, the plebeians refused to come. Instead, they met outside Rome and refused to join the army until the patricians granted them some form of representation. This event is known as the First Secession of the Plebs. The patricians had no choice but to make concessions. They gave the plebeians the right to form the Concilium Plebis and to choose their officials – the tribunes – to protect their rights. This was a first major victory of the plebs, but their position was still far from perfect. The patricians still controlled the law (there was no written legal code at the time; the patricians preserved customary unwritten law and judged by it) and the plebeians were still exposed to exploitation. The first written law called the Twelve Tables was composed in 450 BC, because of the revolt against arbitrary patrician justice. The plebeians could know the law for the first time in Roman history, and their position increasingly improved.

The Twelve Tables had some awkward details. Mixing the classes was, for example, strictly forbidden. Intermarriage between patricians and plebeians was not allowed. Some more important laws were passed in subsequent years. It was no longer possible to enslave a Roman citizen for debt. All citizens were granted the right of *provocatio ad populum*, which meant they could appeal to the people against decisions made by a magistrate. In 449 BC (and again in 287 BC) a law declared the entire population (both the patricians and the plebeians) was to be subject to plebiscites. In 445, the law that forbade intermarriage between the classes was revoked. In the next couple of decades, consuls were frequently replaced by several military tribunes with consular power. In years between 391 and 367, there were six consular tribunes,[19] and plebeians were eligible for election to this function just like patricians.[20] 367 BC brought a series of changes and new laws. In the years that followed, plebeians were frequently elected as consuls, dictators[21], censors, pontiffs, praetors, and augurs. Starting from 342 BC, plebeians had access to nearly all significant political and religious offices. There was still the distinction between the classes by birth, but a new Roman aristocracy emerged. The new ruling class consisted of both patrician and plebeian wealthy families.

As for the poorer plebeians, they were yet to wait for the better times. Their interests were different from those of their leaders. These leaders were men of substantial property, and they aspired to be politically powerful. Wealthy plebeians wanted to contribute to the Roman institutions from which birth excluded them, and they made it. Patrician exclusivity was diminished. Step by step, new reforms, and legislation allowed plebeians to marry patricians and vice versa. The plebeian elite had equal rights as patricians by 300 BC. But the Rome's poor still lived in inadequate conditions, which led to another secession of the plebs – the third and final one – in 287 BC.

A republic took shape when laws had been recorded, and the patricians were enforced to acknowledge plebeian rights, institutions, and organizations. A delicate balance of power had been created, and it worked most of the time. But it did now work flawlessly. Tribunes – the officials of the plebs – had an important power at their discretion: the veto. They could use this power to impede anything against the interests of the plebeians. However, those of plebeians who were wealthy and powerful enough to get themselves elected as tribunes had the interests that were similar to the ones of patricians, rather than the ones of underprivileged plebeians. The reforms we've just mentioned were just a step towards the maturity of the republic, which fully developed during the next two centuries.

Everyday Lives of Ordinary Romans in the Republic

The highest and most sacred duty of all free Roman men, whether patricians or plebeians, was the one toward their country. They were obliged to enter military service whenever needed; accordingly, going to war and coming back home in victory was the highest honor that brought social prestige and glory. Saving the state from peril and increasing its glory and wealth was deeply ingrained in Roman ethos. Military achievements were also the most convenient way for the plebeians to climb up the social ladder and become novi homines, or new men – that is, to become senators or even consuls, endowing their families with newly forged nobility. That is the reason why Roman social hierarchy was not so stiff and rigid as it was in most other ancient societies. That is probably one of the reasons for Rome's political and military supremacy in its brightest days. When the Empire started to collapse, many Romans interpreted it because of utter moral degradation within the nobility and their putting personal interest and wealth before their office and service to the state.

Citizenship was not taken for granted in the Roman Republic. On the contrary, it was a public display of one's merit. Only property-owning males could be citizens and have the right to vote. However, non-citizens performed a significant role in Rome's economy. Slaves brought from Roman military conquests were a large machinery that performed all menial duties, farmed lands, maintained wealthy homes, educated patrician children, labored in mines. Hundreds of thousands of slaves were brought from foreign campaigns. According to some historians, it was precisely the reliance on slaves that hindered Rome's technological improvement and contributed to its downfall. However, Romans took advantage of the diversity within their slave caste; educated war prisoners were held as educators, teachers, and domestic servants, whereas those who were regarded as barbarians were committed to heavy physical labor on farms and in mines. Through exceptional conduct or some great achievement, slaves could earn the right to freedom, hard as it was to do; however, even then this freedom would not be complete. They would still be obliged to obey their former masters and be loyal to them.

The second sacred locus was family. It incorporated the social status of its members as well as the general Roman ethos which dictated rigid hierarchy. A man's social status and affiliation to a specific family were reflected in his name, fusing his public figure and private identity. On the other hand, women had only one name that was simply derived from their father's second name – for example, the daughter of Publius Cornelius Scipio was simply called Cornelia. The pater familias was the decision maker and absolute master of his household, family, and all other family members, their lives, and liberty. He had legal power and authority over all the family's affairs. He could even kill his wife or children or sell them into slavery without any legal consequences. His ancestors, even dead, were regarded as a significant and active factor in his present; their death masks often hanged from the walls in his home, reminding him of his heritage and duties. The atrium was a unique mix of public and private, as a place where meetings were held, and business was conducted.

Accordingly, upper-class marriage was not a private bond between two people who loved each other. Considering the importance of family, marriage was to enforce the family and contribute to its wellbeing. So, it was regarded as an economic and political matter that was arranged by the elders of the two involved families. Marriages were often arranged between children for the future when they should come of age. Age discrepancy was not a problem; Julius Caesar married his teenage daughter to Pompeus who was a few years his senior to strengthen the two families' political bonds. Grooms would bring their brides to their homes to extend the family line within the nucleus of their heritage – and that was their ancestral home.

Women in Rome

There isn't much of written evidence about women, as they were mainly confined to their homes and domestic roles of wives, daughters and household managers. Even those who were free-born, they were always under the complete authority of their fathers and husbands. Exceptions include the Vestals, virgin priestesses in the temples of Vesta, the goddess of the hearth. Their primary role was to maintain the sacred flame, and so they were widely respected, but also harshly punished if they neglected their duty in any way. Their office was not for a lifetime by definition; they could marry and bear children later in life if they wished. As for regular upper-class women, they usually didn't have property – or if they had, it was entirely at their husbands' disposal. They could inherit money from their fathers, and they were usually given dowry when they married. The dowry was the only female possession that was entirely in her hands to do with it as she pleased. If the husband should have to borrow that money, he was obliged to pay it back to her as soon as the circumstances allowed him.

Patrician women could be highly educated, but most of them never got the chance to demonstrate their worth, not having had a chance to participate in the public life. Even if a woman held public respect and prominence, it was only due to her father's or husband's social standing. For example, the aforementioned Cornelia was widely respected as the daughter of Scipio, the wife of Tiberius Gracchus and subsequently the mother of the Gracchi brothers. As such, she was regarded as a paradigm of woman's virtue in ancient Rome – as a paragon of loyalty, modesty, nobility, and fertility, as a mother of twelve and thus a perfect example of a matron.

Public Life

Public life was extraordinarily vivid and developed in Ancient Rome. It was largely financed by the Senate and wealthy patricians who considered it their duty to build public baths, theaters, amphitheaters for gladiatorial games, to sponsor and organize chariot races and other means of entertainment for the city masses. Public baths were not only built in cities but even in villages and other small communities. Gladiatorial games were very symptomatic of Rome's evolution over the centuries; at first, they were part of funeral ceremonies and included only a few fighters to honor the deceased man. With time, they evolved into large, expensive and extravagant public spectacles financed by emperors and magistrates to earn public favor and popularity. They often lasted even for months, with thousands of gladiators butchering each other and the wild animals in front of enthusiastic spectators.

Religion and rituals permeated all spheres of public and private life. In its major part, it was adopted from the Greeks who had inhabited Italian peninsula in the early days of Rome. Thus, the major god was Jupiter, a Roman version of Zeus and Juno, his wife, derived from Greek Hera. The war god Mars was the equivalent of Greek Ares and Venus for the Greek goddess of love and beauty Aphrodite. But there were also many deities adopted from other cultures, such as Sabine Quirinus, who was regarded as the god of the Roman state. All major political and military decisions were followed by sacrifices to the gods, seeking their approval, protection, and blessing; March, as the first month of the year, was brimming with festivals to celebrate the opening of the new season of war campaigns. Romans' everyday life was also infused with the influence of minor spirits who were believed to be the guardians of their homes – such as Lares and Penates. Every household had a small sanctuary devoted to those spirits. Rituals were considered the most important way to summon the gods and connect with them. To foresee the future, Roman priests (*augures* and *haruspices*) watched the skies observing the weather conditions, the birds' flight and examined the entrails of sacrificed animals, much like the Etruscans used to do. To maintain the pax deorum (the peace of the gods) and bring the gods to their side, they held annual festivals, in which all of the citizens participated.

Chapter 4 – Military Achievements of Early Republic: Taking Italy

Rome was in an almost constant state of war – just as were other Italian cities and states. That is why the secessions of plebs had such profound results: Rome needed these men to perform their military service.

The Roman army fought first against the neighboring tribes, Etruscans, Samnites, and others within Italy. In the ages that were yet to come, the Romans dominated the Mediterranean and places as distant as Britannia and Asia Minor. But at the beginning, Rome simply needed to secure its borders and maintain internal order during civil wars.

The Romans did not start off with a master-plan on how to conquer the world. The first wars in the early Roman Republic were mostly of defense. Rome protected itself from surrounding cities and peoples, but it also established its territory in the region.[22] At the very beginning of the Republic, Etruscan armies attacked Rome twice. The overthrown king Tarquin the Proud was Etruscan, and he initiated these attacks to reclaim his throne, or to avenge the people of Rome who expelled him. The Romans fought bravely and won. The Romans' defense impressed and inspired other Latin cities and in (approx.) 506 BC they created the Latin League, determined to get rid of the Etruscans for good. Thirty cities (excluding Rome) collaborated and fought together. The Etruscans attacked the League as soon as it was formed, but with no success. The joint effort worked; the League cut the Etruscans off from southern Italy at the Battle of Aricia and weakened the Etruscans permanently.

Despite the shared enemy, the League and Rome were not allies, at least not at the beginning. The reason was obvious – the Latins were not quite happy about Rome's growing power. The two sides fought at Lake Regillus in 496 BC, but the battle ended as soon as it began, due to politics. The Latins needed Rome's help against mountain tribes that were coming down and invading their land. They made a deal and, consequently, the Latin cities became a part of the Roman system.

The Gauls

The new threat came from Gaulish Celts around 390 BC. The Gauls entered northern Italy and menaced the Etruscan city of Clusium. The Etruscans needed help from Rome, and it came. Rome chased off the invaders, but soon after that, a Gaulish army returned, reaching the river Allia just 15 kilometers (approx.) north of Rome. The armies met, and the Gauls won, causing serious damage to the Roman army, land, and economy. This was a tough lesson for Rome, but substantial for its maturing. A series of economic and political changes took place, and the influence of the plebs increased further. The Roman citizenship was given to many newcomers, as well as ex-slaves (who had no voting rights, but their children did). At the same time, the importance of military service had been additionally highlighted. The Romans were determined to repair the damage and grow strong again. They learned their lesson well and decided that no one would ever capture Rome again. Massive walls[23] were built to prevent anyone from invading the city. When the Gauls came to invade Rome again in 360 BC, they couldn't penetrate the walls and, after a while just turned back home. The construction of the walls was not the only Roman means of defense. They restructured the army entirely to make it more capable of resisting a high-speed barbarian attack. Small, flexible units replaced cumbersome infantry. Troops were armed with javelins and swords. From a merely defensive force, the Roman army grew to become a threatening force. So, when the Etruscans, encouraged by the Gauls' invasion of 360 BC, tried to invade Rome again, the Romans – now the regional leaders – reorganized the Latin League and defeated Etruscans once for all.

The Samnites

The Romans and the Latins were situated in the plains west of the Apennine Mountains, which were the home to several tribes collectively known as the Samnites. They entered each other's territories, and the clash was inevitable. Fearing from another Gaulish invasion, the two sides signed a treaty in 354 BC, but they were not allies for long. When the Samnites began pestering the Campanian city of Capua, Capuans asked Rome for help. The Romans were enthusiastic about the chance to gain the control over the whole region of Campania, so they turned sides and scared away the Samnites from Capua and the surrounding area. The so-called First Samnite War lasted from 343 to 341 BC and ended without a winner. Neither the Romans nor the Samnites could persist and keep fighting. Both sides needed to cope with their problems. The Romans had to deal with a mutiny within the army because the soldiers were not willing to be away from home for such a long time. The Samnites, on the other hand, were exposed to attacks from Tarentum, a Greek colony in southern Italy. The treaty between the Romans and the Samnites was renewed, but another threat was on the way. The Latins saw a chance in the Roman's army mutiny, made an alliance with the Campanians and the Volsci, and demanded the reinstatement of equality between themselves and Rome. But the Romans were not as vulnerable as they seemed. They used their agreement with the Samnites to overwhelm both the Latins and Campanians. After that, the Romans made a deal with the Campanians and, finally, pulled the Latin League apart. The technique called divide and rule – turning one tribe against another – was the Romans' specialty. Each city that used to be a part of the Latin League was forced to face Rome individually and accept a profound change in their status. In 338 BC, they all became the municipiae (municipalities) or colonies of Rome. These cities preserved their identities and partial local autonomy, but their inhabitants became a part of the Roman legislative system.

The mighty Romans made a deal with the Greek city of Tarentum, which was, an enemy to the Samnites. The Samnites then made peace with Tarentum, attacked the Greek port of Neapolis and indirectly threatened the Capuans who, in turn, asked Rome for help. The Romans came, and the Second Samnite War began in 326 BC. The Samnite garrison had to give up their plan to invade the plains of the western coast, and they returned to Samnium. Nothing significant happened during the next couple of years, but the tension persisted. The Romans felt incapable of fighting in the Samnites' mountain terrain. The Samnites, on the other hand, could not do anything on the plains, weighed down by Roman garrisons. In 321 BC the Romans, eager to fight, directed their garrisons from Capua to attack the Samnites on their land. The Roman army was on the way to Samnium, but the Samnites trapped them and forced them into surrender. The Samnites believed they'd won. However, the Romans quickly regrouped. This was one of the greatest Roman advantages; after each defeat, their army grew larger and strategies enhanced. In 316 BC the Samnites won another battle, but in 314 BC returned the control over the territory around the Mountains. In 304 BC peace was made, but in 298 BC the Third Samnite War began, and it lasted for nearly a decade. The Samnites had the support of the Etruscans and the Gauls. It had been hard to fight such a serious enemy, and the Romans lost battle after battle, but eventually, they managed to kill the Samnite leader Egnatius Gellus. The likely disaster turned out to be the Roman triumph. They made allies first with the Samnite helpers, and at the end with the Samnites – under the Romans' conditions, of course. To be a Roman ally meant to be obliged to contribute to Rome's army.

The Greeks

The Romans gradually gained control of most of Italy. The last to deal with was southern Italy or Magna Graecia ('Great Greece') controlled by the Greek colonies, including Tarentum. The Tarentines were wealthy. Their thriving economy enabled them to handle a huge army. They also had a large navy and could even afford mercenaries to help them when needed. In 334 BC, the rulers of Tarentum hired Alexander of Epirus[24] to help them to resist invasions by the Samnites and Lucanians. Alexander turned out to be more interested in appropriating his own empire, and the Tarentines were not particularly moved when the Lucanians killed him.

The Romans were ambitious, and the Tarentines were worried. Rome's power and influence were enormous. Whenever some place felt under threat, they asked the Romans for help. So, when the Romans sent their ships to a nearby Greek city of Thurii, the Tarentines attacked and overwhelmed them. They were feeling self-assured because they had employed the number one Greek soldier of his day, King Pyrrhus of Epirus, and his army of 25,000 men and 20 war elephants, which were borrowed by the Egyptian ruler Ptolemy II. Pyrrhus won in 280 BC at Heraclea, and again in 279 BC, at Asculum, but it was a costly victory with large loses. From Pyrrhus's perspective, it wasn't worth it. So, he went to fight the Carthaginians instead. Meanwhile, the Romans attacked the Samnites and the Lucanians, who in 276 BC asked Pyrrhus to return and help them. He came, but the Romans defeated him at Beneventum. Aside from the expression 'Pyrrhus's victory,' meaning a victory that just wasn't worth it, Pyrrhus is remembered by his extraordinary death. After all those battles and wars, he participated in, he died by accident, when a pot flanged out of a window fell on his head.

Pyrrhus was history, and the world of possibilities was open for the Romans. In 272 BC they seized Tarentum, and finally gained control of the entire Italian peninsula. All Greek cities had no choice but to enter the Roman system and become *socii* (allies). Just like the Latin cities had to provide troops, the Greek cities provided ships. The peninsula now consisted of Roman colonies.

The Roman supremacy did not go unnoticed by the other powerful armies on the Mediterranean, and both the Carthaginians and the Egyptians were making deals of friendship with the Roman Republic.

Chapter 5 – Middle Republic: The Punic Wars and Mediterranean Dominance

By 275 BC the Roman Republic was firmly established and its political and social structures fully defined. The joint leadership of the Senate granted stability and directed the ambitions of the elite. The populace had a voice through assemblies and elections. In return, the ordinary Romans willingly contributed to military campaigns. The large network of Roman allies, ranging from the nearby Latin cities and tribes to the ones on the south, previously known as Magna Graecia, enlarged the Rome's power and gave it control over all of Italy. However, the Republic was still just a regional player, not a Mediterranean one. But this changed during the 3rd century BC. The expansion of Roman prospects outside Italy got Rome into direct conflict with a terrifying enemy – Carthage in North Africa. Rome fought against Carthage in the Punic War between 264 and 146 BC. The Roman Republic was almost destroyed in dramatic twists and turns, but it won in the end, becoming a genuine Mediterranean power.

The Phoenicians (*Punici*) and Carthage

Ancient Carthage has been thoroughly ruined, and we know nothing about their point of view regarding the Punic wars. We interpret their motives and actions through the historical texts written by Livy and Polybius.[25] After all, history has always been written by the victors, especially in the ancient times when great civilizations were ruined leaving no written accounts of their own. Hence for us, the Phoenicians were simply the foes of Rome. But thanks to Roman historians, however biased they might be, we know more about this remarkable ancient society.

Carthage was indeed mighty. The city was founded in c. 800 BC by Phoenicians, who came from the eastern city of Tyre (present-day Lebanon) and were specialized in maritime trading. Carthage was located on a first-class natural harbor on the cape that today belongs to the city of Tunis. Carthage controlled entire trade in the western Mediterranean, and according to Polybius, was 'the richest city in the world.' Its moneymaking empire spread across North Africa, into Spain, and (then Greek, now Italian) islands of Sardinia and Sicily.

While Rome relied primarily on agriculture, the people of Carthage were devoted to trade and industry. The political and military structures of the two sides were equally different. Rome was, as we have elaborated, a fully developed republic, and Carthage was an oligarchy, with its wealthiest families at the top. Its army consisted of mercenaries – Numidia's elite cavalry and even North African elephants – directed by Carthaginian officers. Carthage particularly relied on its remarkable navy, roughly 200 *quinquiremes*, magnificent, 45 meters long galleys, each carrying 120 battle marines. With such impressive and efficient navy and well-trained men, Carthage controlled the western Mediterranean for years. And then the Romans emerged.

The First Punic War

As the Roman Republic grew stronger, a rivalry with Carthage was inevitable. The two forces were in good terms with each other at the beginning; they even signed a treaty during the Pyrrhic war. This alliance was a useful means against Pyrrhus's aggression, but after he was defeated the things changed drastically. Rome now controlled all of Italy including its southmost area and, naturally, its activities spread on Sicily, which was under the Carthaginian domain. For centuries Carthage fought against the Syracusan and other Greeks to achieve dominance. But now a band of Italian mercenaries called *the sons of Mars* (*Mamertines*) conquered the Sicilian city of Messina and attacked both Carthaginian and Syracusan territory. The attacks started in 288 BC, and in 265 BC opposing factions within Messina asked Rome and Carthage for help. Carthage sent a fleet, but a Roman army came into Sicily and forced the Carthaginian commander to surrender the town. Syracuse joined Rome against Carthage, and thus the First Punic War began in 264 BC.

Rome's ambitions

It is easy to understand why the Carthaginians sent a fleet to help Messina; they had a long history of involvement in the region. But why did the Romans come? There are several possible answers. Rome might have been frightened by the prospects of the Carthaginians' dominance in Sicily. Or they were driven by *fides* (good faith) and felt they needed to support their allies in times of danger. According to ancient sources – including the contemporary Romans themselves – they fought only in defense of either their city or their friends. But was that all? There was also the fact the Romans just loved war. Its society appreciated the economic rewards of conquest, and the elite fought for military glory. The consuls personally led the armies and the Senate, which made all the decisions and pushed Rome towards warfare.

Fighting at sea

After the opening clash over Messina, both sides were idle for a while. Carthage was focused on defending the coastal towns, and the Romans couldn't approach them from the land. Meanwhile, the Carthaginian navy started attacking the Italian coast. The Romans had a few ships, but not a proper navy, and now was the perfect time to start constructing one. So, they did it. Within 60 days, the Romans built 120 quinquiremes. The Romans themselves did not have much experience at sea, but the allies from southern Italy did, so they became the crew of new Roman ships. In 260 BC at Mylae, the Rome's fleet achieved a great victory. They captured 50 Carthage ships and demolished them; the bronze was used to decorate a column in the Roman Forum in honor of Gaius Duilius.

Rome had suddenly become a serious naval force, and then everything changed. The Romans recognized an opportunity, and in 256-255 BC sent an army to Africa to attack Carthage, but without success. Carthaginian mercenaries led by the Spartan Xanthippus crushed the Roman army, and the support from the sea got caught in a severe storm, 280 ships with over 100,000 men were lost. More fleets fell victims to storms in the following years; the Carthaginians beat others. The war was long and exhaustive, both sides suffered substantial losses, and neither was winning. The consequences were felt in Rome. Roughly 20 percent of Italian men had passed away, either in battles or storms. Nevertheless, Rome was unwilling to discuss peace. Instead, the legislative institutions raised the taxes and ordered the aristocrats to give loans with no exceptions. Every three senators had to provide a warship. As a result, a brand-new fleet was built. In 241 BC, close to the Aegates Islands (which belonged to western Sicily), this fleet won a final naval victory. The war was over, and the Carthaginians were forced to leave Sicily and pay reparation of 3,200 silver talents (roughly one hundred tons of silver). Carthage was economically devastated, and its mercenaries revolted. Meanwhile, the Romans took Sardinia, and then requested 1,200 talents from Carthage, or else they would restart the war.

The end of the First Punic War additionally confirmed Rome's power. The Roman Republic proved itself to be resilient in hard times, able to deal with both military and economic pressure. Moreover, the net of Roman allies functioned well. The loyalty had been confirmed, and the links strengthened. As for Sicily, it became the first tax-paying province of Rome. This was not the only difference in status between Sicily and Roman ally cities in Italy. A Roman praetor must govern this area, and a Roman quaestor got the job to oversee taxation. A small garrison stayed there as well, just in case. Other than that, the social and political structures were preserved. The Romans developed a highly flexible system in which political structures of a province remained virtually intact, while Rome ruled through the local elites. This became the standard for all provincial administration under the Roman Republic. Sicily was first, next was Sardinia, and many other places and cities were yet to become Roman provinces.

The Second Punic War: Hannibal and Scipio

After Carthage lost Sicily and Sardinia, its leaders focused on expanding its territory in Spain. The Carthaginians exploited the precious Spanish silver mines to pay the tax that Rome demanded. Spain was under the rule of the Carthaginian general Hamilcar Barca (*Thunderer*) who passionately hated the Romans and sought revenge, as well as restoring Carthaginian dignity. He raised a son teaching him to hate the Romans too. At the age of nine, the young Hannibal swore that he would forever be the foe of Rome. Hannibal was the greatest single enemy that the Republic ever encountered.[26] According to Livy, he was one of the best generals of ancient times; a leader that inspired confidence in his men; both mentally and physically strong; brave and resilient; "unequalled as a fighting man, always the first to attack, the last to leave the field."[27] Livy clearly admired him, but he also pointed out that Hannibal's dark side was just as impressive as his virtues, and highlighted his "inhuman cruelty, [...] perfidy, a total disregard of truth, honor, and religion."[28]

Hannibal led the Carthaginian army into the Second Punic War. It wasn't just a hate campaign driven by his wish for revenge. Rome was alarmed by Carthage's expansion into Spain. The 226 BC treaty fixed the River Ebro as the border between the spheres of interest, but then Rome formed an agreement of friendship with the town of Saguntum, which belonged to the Carthaginian sphere. The war had been provoked by Hannibal's attack upon Saguntum in 219 BC. Rome required Hannibal to surrender, but the request was declined, so the Second Punic War began in 218 BC.

Rome and Carthage had different ideas about where the fighting was going to start. The Romans were preparing to attack Carthaginian land in both Spain and North Africa, but

Hannibal had already started marching for the Alps. His idea was to invade Italy, Rome's source of men and resources. His way was risky; he needed to cross the Alpine mountains, during which more than half his men and a number of elephants died. But Hannibal was determined. He managed to enter Italy with his finest warriors, and then the Gauls from Cisalpine (the town that had just been added to the Roman system and wasn't entirely happy about it) joined him.

Hannibal's triumphs; the battle at Cannae

Hannibal inflicted huge losses on the Romans in Italy. First, in November 218 BC, his Numidian cavalry won a battle at the River Ticinus because the Roman army led by the consul Sempronius Longus was late and didn't have a chance to fight. Once the Romans finally arrived, in December, they attacked the Carthaginians at the River Trebia and were devastated. 20,000 Romans died, Hannibal proclaimed victory and the 'liberation' of Rome's allies and released all his Italian prisoners (those from the Roman "ally" cities) without ransom. The Romans didn't care about his propaganda and attacked him again in the spring. Gaius Flaminius, one of that year's (217 BC) elected consuls, led the army, which pursued the Carthaginians through Etruria, and then fell into a trap at the Lake Trasimene. Hannibal's cavalry came from the back and cut the Romans off. 15,000 men, including Flaminius, were either killed in conflict or drowned. This situation required special measures. Rome appointed a dictator, Quintus Fabius Maximus. His nickname Cunctator means 'Delayer.', His strategy included avoiding open battle and finding a way to make Hannibal exhausted. This strategy was profoundly different from the Roman style of fighting, and Fabius had no support within his lines, so he was unable to prevent Hannibal entering southern Italy. In 216 BC, the newly elected consuls, Lucius Aemilius Paullus and Gaius Terentius Varro led the Roman forces to encounter Hannibal at Cannae. This battle was the greatest Republican defeat for over a century.[29] Even though there were two times more Romans than Carthaginians, Hannibal managed to encircle, trap and slaughter them. Hannibal then continued advancing and was only six miles from Rome.

The Battle of Cannae was Hannibal's greatest success that assured his reputation as a military genius. Now his propaganda began to have an effect, and he won over many of Rome's allies, mostly the Greek colonies in southern Italy and Syracuse in Sicily. However, he still had no sufficient power to attack the city of Rome itself. Also, he failed to win over all of Rome's allies; most Italian people and cities remained loyal to Rome.

The changes in Roman tactics

Meanwhile, in Rome, it became clear the Republican system of annually elected magistrates didn't work at war. Fabius Maximus Cunctator was restored to power together with the aggressive

Marcus Claudius Marcellus. They became known as the 'Shield and Sword of Rome.' Rome was recovering. Up to that point, the Carthaginians had killed over 70,000 Romans in a short period of just three years. But by 212 BC, a new army of 200,000 Roman soldiers in Italy, Sicily, and Spain was ready to confront Hannibal. Approximately 50,000 men were positioned only to stalk Hannibal's army, which was hugely outnumbered. The Romans had the mission to restrict the Carthaginians' progressing and suppress those who joined their side. The Romans were determined to win this war.

Hannibal's movements in Italy were restricted, and Rome's army won some great victories attention. Marcellus regained Roman control over Syracuse in 211 BC, and soon after that, over entire Sicily, but got killed in 208 in Italy by another of Hannibal's surprise attacks. It felt like victory for the Carthaginians, so they made a major attempt to strengthen Hannibal's army. A relief force led by Hannibal's brother Hasdrubal came close but was crashed at the River Metaurus in 207 BC. Hasdrubal was murdered and his head thrown into Hannibal's camp. Meanwhile, decisive events were taking place on another front - in Spain.

Rome's new blood: Scipio Africanus

While Hannibal was kept busy in Italy, two Roman generals, the brothers Publius and Gnaeus Cornelius Scipio led an army that opened a series of attacks upon Carthage's possessions in Spain. When 211 BC the Carthaginians killed them in battle, Publius's son also named Publius Cornelius Scipio took over as head of the army. Something like that never happened before in the history of Rome. The young Scipio was only 24 years old. Not only had he never held a public office; he was still ineligible to apply for a position of authority. On the other hand, he was brave, an excellent soldier, and unusually popular within the Roman society.

Scipio instantly restructured the forces in Spain. He introduced new weapons like the Spanish short sword called the gladius and the pilum. Moreover, he reorganized the Roman legion and made its formation more flexible. This new army was highly efficient at the rough terrain of Spain and would shortly prove equally successful against inflexible Greek phalanx. Scipio and his men crossed 250 miles in only five days and attacked the unsuspecting Carthaginians at Nova Carthago (modern Cartagena). Scipio realized the town's fortifications were weak on the coastal side, so he crossed the water at low tide and conquered Nova Carthago in 209 BC. Rome, therefore, took the control over the abundant silver mines close to the city. By 205 BC, Carthaginian forces had been expelled from Spain.

Scipio returned home in 205 BC, welcomed as the true hero of Rome. Thanks to immense popularity and public support, despite the objections of older senators led by Fabius Maximus, he became a consul and got chosen to lead the previously planned Roman invasion of North

Africa. Hannibal had to return to his city after 30 years, to defend it from the Romans. The Romans, on the other side, managed to win the support of the Numidians, despite their historic alliance with Carthage. Scipio's army won the victory in the final battle of Zama in 202 BC. The Romans did not destroy the city of Carthage, but it was severely damaged, and its power was diminished. This was the greatest Roman victory so far. In commemoration of this remarkable triumph, Publius Cornelius Scipio took the name Africanus.

The aftermath of the Second Punic War

The Second Punic War confirmed once again the strength of the Roman Republic and the extraordinary loyalty of its Italian allies. Hannibal was indeed an incomparable military genius, but even he could not compete with the resilience of the Romans. Rome could absorb the losses and continue fighting until it won. But that does not mean there were no consequences the people of Rome were forced to endure. Numerous people died, families suffered, and so did Rome's dominant industry – agricultural production. At the same time, the increasing wealth the Roman expansion brought caused internal instability within the Republic in the following century.

Scipio Africanus represented a large change in the Roman establishment. His authority and military glory overshadowed the Senate. He became a consul at the age of 30. He had never met the formal criteria, as he never held a junior governmental position. Moreover, he was given command ahead of the aristocrats from the previous generation, like Fabius Maximus. Scipio's extraordinary achievement made him hard to compete against. And many were yet to try, including Julius Caesar and Emperor Augustus.

The end of Carthage

Rome came into conflict with Carthage one final time in the 2nd century BC. This conflict is sometimes called Third Punic War, but it was just a sad epilogue to their decades of rivalry. Carthage was partially recovering until 195 BC when the Romans requested Hannibal's extradition. To avoid extradition, Hannibal went into exile. That was not the worst thing that happened to the Carthaginians. All military activities were forbidden for them because those were the terms of Carthage's surrender to Rome. Numidia abused this terms by continually seizing Carthaginian territory. The Carthaginians asked Rome for help several times, but the appeal was rejected every time. After the complete indemnity had been paid to Rome, in 151 BC, Carthage fought Numidia. Shortly after that, a Roman embassy led by Marcus Porcius Cato, the Elder arrived to investigate the issue. Upon returning to Rome, Cato declared that Carthage posed a significant danger to Rome and should be destroyed. His famous words *Carthage must be destroyed* (*Carthago delenda est*) became the conclusion of his every speech in the Senate. As a result, Rome again sent its forces to Carthage in 149 BC. The Carthaginians consented to every request, released 300 hostages and handed over all their weapons. This was still not enough for the Romans. They demanded the Carthaginians leave their homes. They were supposed to build a new city at least 10 miles from the sea. This was too much for the unfortunate people of Carthage, so they started fighting out of desperation and endured, with enormous effort, for three years. The annoyed Romans chose another underage consul – the adopted grandson of Scipio Africanus, Publius Cornelius Scipio Aemilianus – who finally broke and destroyed Carthage, and enslaved all surviving people. The Romans went even further; they cursed the ground that used to be Carthage and sowed it with salt. Finally, entire North Africa became a province of the Roman Republic.

Chapter 6 – The Military vs. Cultural Dominance: The Roman Civilization meets the Greek World

After the spectacular triumph over Carthage, the Roman Republic became the leading power of the western Mediterranean. It ruled over entire Italy, Sicily, Sardinia, Spain, and North Africa. But its influence wasn't limited by the borders of its provinces. The Roman Republic oppressed the neighboring areas through political, economic, and military supremacy. Some minor tribes still resisted the influence of Rome, but after Carthage had fallen, no enemy posed a direct threat to the Republic.

In the ancient Mediterranean, the centers of power used to be in the east. The Greek city-states were not nearly as powerful anymore as they were in their best ages, but the sophistication of any civilization was still measured by comparing to the Greek standard. The Greek language, culture, art, philosophy, and literature confirmed Greek's cultural dominance.

After the conquests of Alexander the Great, the eastern part of the Mediterranean had been split between an always changing number of cities, kingdoms, and leagues. Naturally, during the 2nd century BC, the entire Hellenistic world had to admit the domination of the Romans. Rome's relationship with Greece was twofold. The Romans admired Greek culture, which thoroughly influenced and refined the Roman world. The fascination with all things Greek existed for centuries. The Etruscans respected and widely copied them. King Tarquin, the Elder on one occasion, sent his sons to the oracle in Delphi for advice. In subsequent centuries, numerous Greek statues were brought to Rome. Even Roman pantheon was altered to match with the Greek gods. Greek literature was translated into Latin, and so on. Greek freedom, on the other hand, was not respected that much and Roman armies crushed those who tried to preserve it.

Greece after Alexander the Great

Alexander the Great died in 323 BC. Before his death, he expressed the last will; he wanted his vast conquests to be ruled by 'the strongest.' That was not one of his best decisions. The empire he built over decades was immediately crushed, thanks to the forces from inside. Alexander's generals, each wanting to be 'the strongest,' fought for control. The empire had become fragmented. Three kingdoms arose in its place: the Antigonid dynasty ruled Macedon, Syria under the Seleucids and Egypt under the Ptolemies. Greece was governed by unions of allied cities. The Aetolian League controlled the area north of the Corinthian Gulf. Peloponnese was under control of the Achaean League. Major Greek city-states, such as Athens and Sparta, as well as few others, remained independent, but their political importance was significantly reduced over the centuries. There were a few more states within the territory of what once was the Alexander's empire, including the island of Rhodes and Pergamum in Asia Minor. These cities had a long history of wars and alliances, many of which Rome was utterly unaware.

The Romans come to Greek territory

Military and politically, no individual Greek state could compare with the Roman Republic. But this time it was not all about brute power. The Greek east had a highly sophisticated culture, and the Romans respected that. The Greeks were acknowledged as the arbiters of civilization. This made things complicated for the Romans. They did not want merely to invade the Hellenistic world and be seen as barbarians. They wanted to be part of the civilized world. This aspiration influenced Roman behavior and tactic. As a result, the process of conquering the eastern Mediterranean was long and, at moments, very painful.

The armies of the two worlds had met before. The Greek ruler Pyrrhus from Epirus invaded Italy in the early 3rd century BC. Roma managed to resist. Now, after the history of defeating threatening forces from the east – first Pyrrhus's, then Hannibal's army, the Romans directed their attention toward that side of the world. The first conflicts began between the two great Punic Wars when Rome invaded the coastal region of Illyria. Philip V, ruler of the nearby kingdom of Macedon, saw the Romans as a threat (the Illyrian pirates were, after all, his mercenaries) and, after the battle of Cannae, he signed a treaty of cooperation with Hannibal. The so-called First Macedonian War ended quickly – Philip realized Rome was going to win the Second Punic War and signed peace in 205 BC – but two years after they crushed Carthage, the Roman authorities declared war on Macedon. Thus, began the Second Macedonian War.

Rome, Macedon and the freedom of Greece

There were many reasons for Rome to enter the war against Macedon. Philip V, supported by the Seleucid Empire in Syria, wanted to attack Egypt and take power and the wealth away from the underage king Ptolemy V. On the way, Philip's forces harassed everyone else in the Aegean. The Greeks got upset by his actions. Pergamon and Rhodes allied with Philip who, in turn, hammered their joined forces. In 201 BC those Greeks asked Rome for help. But, curiously enough, the people of Rome did not want to fight. The first consul's request for a declaration of war against Macedon was declined in 200 BC by the Comitia Centuriata. Even the Roman elite, which was always eager to fight and attain military glory, was reluctant. But once the word had spread that Phillip was in alliance with the Seleucids, the war was inevitable. The Romans wanted to crush Antiochus the Great of the Seleucids, along with Philip, but they made it look as if their only goal was to protect the Greek cities.

Greeks warmly welcomed the Roman legions. The Aetolian and Achaean Leagues united and stood behind Rome. However, at first, it looked like Philip was winning, but the joint Greek-Roman army led by Titus Quinctius Flamininus managed to defeat the Macedonians at the end. Like Scipio Africanus, Flaminius was only 30 years old. He was a philhellene, an admirer of Greek culture who spoke Greek fluently, and a man capable of winning Greek support and promoting an appropriate image of Rome as a civilized state.

At the Isthmian Games of Corinth in 196 BC, Flamininus gave a speech in Greek and proclaimed the 'Freedom of Greece.' The Greeks were so happy that, as later Roman sources say, their intense shout of joy killed the flying ravens.[30] Greeks were so grateful and went so far they honored Flamininus as a god.

At this point, the Romans respected Greek freedom. Rome had withdrawn all its troops by 194 BC. Greek cities did not become new Roman provinces. This was very unusual, but there were two reasons to let Greece alone. First, Rome did not have the resources – either the standing army or the bureaucracy – that would make it possible to administer Greece. And there was also the admiration for Greek culture. Rome initially counted more on diplomacy than direct rule. After all, Greek opinion carried some weight and Rome had to appear 'civilized.' But in 106 BC Rome declared the Greeks were under its protection and hence indirectly challenged Antiochus III of Seleucid Syria, also known as Antiochus the Great. The most prominent of

Hellenistic monarchs, Antiochus was a powerful ruler with imperialistic attitude who continuously frightened Pergamum and Rhodes, which were now Rome's allies. In 195 BC Hannibal, who had been banished from Carthage, joined Antiochus, and this additionally concerned the Romans. Meanwhile, the Aetolian League abandoned the alliance with Rome and joined Antiochus who in 191 BC entered Greece.

Rome reacted instantly and crushed Antiochus at Thermopylae, the famous place where the Spartans had fought against the Persians three centuries earlier. The Seleucid army had to retreat into Syria. The new consul Lucius Cornelius Scipio, followed by his brother Scipio Africanus (Lucius won election thanks to Africanus, who promised to serve alongside him) routed the enemy. Rome once again withdrew its troops from Greece, but its power over eastern territories had been confirmed. Antiochus was ordered to surrender Hannibal who meanwhile disappeared, to be found by Flamininus in 183 BC. The old foe of Rome took the poison, so he wouldn't have to surrender to Rome.

Graeco-Roman culture and the tension

Graecia capta ferum victorem cepit et artes intulit agresti Latio.—Horace[31]

Over the next couple of decades, Rome continued with the same policy toward Greek cities – there were no troops, no tributes, and no provinces. The Greek impact on Roman life, on the other hand, increased dramatically. Greek art and literature flooded into Italy. Roman noble households employed Greek teachers. The new hybrid culture was developing, and philhellenes led by Flamininus and Scipio Africanus encouraged it. But there was another stream within Rome, according to which philhellenism posed a threat to Rome's traditional values. Marcus Porcius Cato the Elder and his supporters believed the Greeks were not only inferior to the Romans, but also a source of corruption.

The Republic adopted their hardline politics around 170 BC. From that time onwards, Rome still appreciated Greek culture but expected the Greeks to acknowledge their authority. The Greek cities were expected to act like Rome's Italian allies – they were 'free' to rule themselves, as long as they remained still and acted only when instructed to do so. The Greeks thought otherwise. The Greeks had a long history of rivalries and local conflicts, and this did not stop with the arrival of Rome. The Senate of the Roman Republic now received numerous appeals and had to act as an arbiter in Greek disputes. This was boring and exhaustive for Roma officials, who started supporting causes randomly. The cases that had something to do with Rome were solved in a way that suited Roman interests. Such was the case of Macedon. Perseus of Macedon was driven into the Third Macedonian War and refused to fight against Romans until his kingdom was crushed, even though he was willing to surrender under any conditions.

Rome still wasn't interested in seizing territories or creating provinces in the east, but the Republic required the recognition of its power. After it destroyed Macedon, others felt the force too. The Romans executed 500 leading Aetolians and took 1,000 Achaeans, including the future historian Polybius, as prisoners. 150,000 people from Epirus were enslaved, The power of Pergamum and Rhodes was significantly reduced. Antiochus IV of Syria was requested to abandon his plans of invading Ptolemaic Egypt, and he had no choice but to conform to the will of Rome.

By 167 BC, no one could challenge Roman power. Polybius advised his fellow Greeks to abide by Roman dominance and avoid experiencing 'the fate that awaited those who opposed Rome.'[32] He was correct. All later revolts were brutally crushed. Macedonia finally became a Roman province. Corinth was destroyed in 146 BC, the same year when Carthage faced the same destiny. The days of 'freedom' given to the Greeks in Corinth half a century before were over. Greece, Syria, and Egypt were still not Rome's provinces (but would become so under Augustus), but the Roman Republic effectively ruled over the Greek city-states and the legacy of Alexander the Great.

Chapter 7 – Limitless Power and the Beginning of the End: The Late Republic

By 130s BC, Rome conquered the whole Mediterranean. This was an astonishing achievement. There is no state, ancient or modern, in the world that ever managed to get even close to that. Other ancient societies controlled significantly smaller territories. The Egyptians at the peak of their power weren't much influential beyond the areas of Levant and Asia Minor. The Greeks had many colonies around the Mediterranean, but they lacked centralized control and a well-structured political system that would hold everything together. Romans not only beat them all politically and militarily. It was them, not the Greeks, who spread Greek art, literature, and philosophy all over the world.

At the end of the century, Rome was the most powerful state in the ancient world and beyond. But within another century, the Roman Republic was gone. Those were the years of ambition, corruption, and civil war that threatened to destroy all that had been achieved over the previous centuries. The rich grew richer, the poor became even poorer, and the traditional institutions could not cope with the new challenges.

The origin of crisis

The Roman Republican system was initially established around public services, like consulship. Ideally, because people were elected for public functions year after year, no one individual was supposed to become pre-eminent. It didn't function that way. Individuals could not hold power for a long time, but their families could. The elite that, as we've seen, included the patricians and the most successful plebeian families (*nobiles*), controlled entire political system.

The voting system was seriously flawed. People who lived far away from the city of Rome could not come and vote. As for those who lived inside the city walls, their votes were frequently and routinely bought. The buying of votes was simple. The most powerful individuals called the patrons were surrounded by their *clients*: the ex-slaves that they freed, business associates and other people who needed the protection of a patron. So, the patrons helped and supported their clients, who in turn voted for them without exception. Votes were also bought for cash and through the organization of free public entertainments. As a result, no plebeian could ever enter the Senate.

The angry crowd

Former agricultural workers and smallholders had become soldiers during the times of wars. The problem of workforce in the fields was solved then by bringing slaves. Now the war was over; these men were out of work. The growth of large estates held by the elite and slave labor, small farmers, struggled to keep land of their own. Too many of them were left without anything. Out of desperation, they came to Rome. The growing urban mob was at times hostile and presented a great risk of disorder. The elite that made them poor had to find the way to control them.

There was a similar crisis with the Italian allies. Their people died at battlefields for Rome, and their loyalty was essential for Rome's success, but they received almost nothing in return, and their political influence was heavily limited.

No one wanted to go to war anymore. Both the Romans and the allies tried their best to avoid military service, and this was a large problem, as we will see.

A new class: the equestrians

The very structure of Roman society was changing. Some new wealthy families requested their share of power. The equestrians or equites were initially the knights, Roman citizens rich enough to serve in a cavalry. Meanwhile, they became a separate bloc within the society and a second-grade elite. Even though they did not have the status of old aristocracy, they possessed substantial wealth. From 129 BC, the *ordo equester* was formally separated from the senatorial order, which made it hard (but still possible) for equestrians to become senators. Nevertheless, this social class was involved in lucrative construction projects and the collection of taxes.

The Gracchi

The Gracchi – Tiberius and Gaius Gracchus had the highest aristocratic origin. Their father was the distinguished war commander and was twice elected consul. Their mother Cornelia was the daughter of the Rome's greatest hero, Scipio Africanus. But these noble brothers were determined to reform the same social and political system that had made their families powerful.

Tiberius and Gaius Gracchus made every effort to pass laws that would improve the status of the Roman citizens in Italy and make the distribution of land more just. However, their efforts were against the interest of the Senate and the aristocracy, who used all methods available to weaken them. Eventually, the Gracchi brothers got killed, and the reforms failed. All they managed to do was to make a name for themselves in history as popular Roman martyrs.

Tiberius Sempronius Gracchus, the older of the brothers, was expected to achieve military success and become a consul. But he had other plans. He became a tribune, determined to fight for social justice. In 133 BC, he recommended that abandoned land all around Italy should be given to unemployed small farmers. This measure would solve three acute problems: social tension would be reduced; the urban mob would disperse, and people would be willing to go to army again. But the land he was talking about – the public land taken during conquests – was largely exploited by aristocrats, who employed slaves to work on fields. There was a limitation of how much of the public land could be used by one Roman, and Tiberius wanted to confiscate all land that exceeded that limit and share it among the unemployed people. These properties would be small, but inalienable, and wealthy landowners could not buy them.

The senatorial elite was entirely against this plan. They inherited the public land (paradoxical, but true) for generations and weren't willing to share it with the poor. They used all political power to stop Tiberius, but he brought the law called *Lex Sempronia agrarian*. But this law could not be enforced. Tiberius was alone against many and found himself persistently obstructed.

Meanwhile, King Attalus III of Pergamum died. He had no heirs, and his kingdom now belonged to Rome. Tiberius took this opportunity to subsidize his property redistribution. In a decree in 133 BC, he announced the people – not the government – would govern the new province of Asia. The Roman Republican institutions were challenged, Tiberius was accused of wanting to become a king, which eventually got him killed and thrown into the river Tiber.

In 123 BC, Tiberius' younger brother Gaius won election as tribune. He knew well what he could expect from the senatorial elite, but he, too, pursued the reform that his brother had begun. He also required the redistribution of land to help the small farmers. On the other hand, his ideas were much broader, developed further, and brought prosperity to all levels of Republican society. In the end, he was judged by the Senate, and the first ever final decree of the Senate (senatus consultum ultimum) decided that Gaius' death would in best interest of Rome. His supporters were murdered, and he committed suicide. It was promised that whoever brought Gaius' head would receive its weight in gold. The man who brought the head first took the brain out and filled it with molten lead before requesting the reward. Thus, began the century of chaos, internal tension, and military crisis.

Marius, the first warlord

In 112 BC, Jugurtha, the king of Numidia, and African province of Rome ordered the murder of Roman and Italian traders in the province. This insult caused the beginning of the Jugurthine War. Jugurtha could not compete with Rome military, but he took significant advantage over the corruption and incompetence of Roman generals. According to Jugurtha, Rome was "a city up for sale, and its days are numbered should it find a buyer." The war dragged on until, in 107 BC, Gaius Marius was elected consul and took over command. Marius was known as *a novus homo*. He reached the consulship thanks to his abilities, not his family. He enjoyed a reputation of an experienced soldier, and he beat Jugurtha swiftly. Then a new threat came. Whole tribes of Germans were moving into Roman Territory. Marius fought them successfully, but with enormous casualties. Meanwhile, he reformed the army by letting all volunteers fight. Rome for the first time in history had a permanent army. These new soldiers had neither properties nor obligations at home and could serve for long periods under rigorous discipline. They could not afford to equip themselves since they were poor, so they were all armed alike by the state. Celebrated as the savior of Rome, Marius was elected consul five years in a row. His domination of the consulship was unprecedented status. He became the first in the line of the great warlords who dominated the last decades of the Republic.

The Marian reforms established a professional infantry army, which collided with the old ideal of a Roman citizen militia. The soldiers had no land but were promised a farm at the end of their service. They were loyal to their general, not the Senate. These changes caused the emergence of private armies in the service of men influential enough to keep them. The first to make the advantage of the new possibilities was Lucius Cornelius Sulla, Marius's long-time rival.

The war against allies: The Social War

The status of Rome's Italian allies had not been improved over the years, and they still had no political rights. On the other hand, two-thirds of Marius' soldiers were Italians, not Roman citizens. They demanded Italian Roman citizenship and, when in 91 BC their defender, the tribune Marcus Livius Drusus, was murdered, they initiated the Social War (the Latin term for 'allies' was 'socii'). Their aim was not to demolish Rome but to demand concessions and in 88 BC Rome finally submitted to the demands and war was over.

Sulla's march on Rome

The leading Roman general in this war was Sulla, and at the end of the war, he was elected consul. Then a new enemy emerged – king Mithridates of Pontus on the Black Sea. Sulla led an army to repel Mithridates' offensive on the Roman province of Asia, but just when the army was to leave, Sulpicius Rufus, a radical tribune, managed to pass a law that shifted the command from Sulla to Marius. Sulla appealed to his men to fight to defend his dignity, and they did. Those men were loyal to him personally, not to the senate, and depended upon him for the properties they had been promised. The Senate had no authority over the warlord with his private army. The Republic's destiny was now in the hands of individuals whose competitive ethos and determination for supremacy could not be limited. The collapse of the Republic had begun.

Chapter 8 – The Age of the Generals: Pompeius, Crassus, and Caesar

The Republic sunk even further after Sulla's death. The shape of Roman history in the following decades was defined by three generals – Gnaeus Pompeius, Marcus Licinius Crassus, and Gaius Julius Caesar. Each of them led an army. They competed for power. Depending on the circumstances they sometimes worked together, sometimes against each other. And they were all brutally killed.

Gnaeus Pompeius

Pompey was born an equestrian, the son of a general. He bravely fought alongside his father in many battles, including the one for Sulla against Marius. His bravery, appearance, and manners granted him enormous popularity. In Africa, where he fought Marius's supporters, he earned the title Magnus (the Great). In Spain, he defeated Sertorius. Maybe the most famous war he participated in was the slave war. From 73 to 71 BC a massive number of slaves from Italy under the gladiator Spartacus revolted. They were well-armed, well-prepared, and not easy to deal with. The general who defeated them was Marcus Licinius Crassus, but Pompey returned from Spain at the very end of the war and claimed all the glory. In 67 BC Pompey crushed the Sicilian pirates in the eastern Mediterranean.

Pompey and Crassus hated each other, but they realized they would be immensely powerful if they worked together. In 70 BC, they became joint consuls. They returned to the tribunes all the authority they had before Sulla's rule. Now they knew they could count on the tribunes in case the Senate tried to make them give up their armies.

In 66 BC, Pompey defeated Mithridates VI, King of Pontus, while he was still around, subjugated Armenia, Syria, and Judaea in 62 BC. Then he did something extraordinary: he established colonies, gave the land to the pirates so they would have something useful to do, and set up a king in Judaea who became his loyal client. Then he returned home and dismissed his army, requiring the Senate to approve his settlement and the land for his veterans. But the only way to achieve this was to join with Crassus and Julius Caesar in the First Triumvirate.

Marcus Licinius Crassus

Crassus was also the son of a general who fought against Marius. He joined Sulla in Italy in 83 BC and was given the reward was to increase his wealth dealing with of Sulla's proscriptions against his enemies. However, Crassus often added innocent people to the list, so he could confiscate their estate. Thus, he lost Sulla's trust but was still popular with the people. Crassus served as praetor, then general, and defeated Spartacus. He hated Pompey for taking the credit but cooperated with him.

Julius Caesar

Gaius Julius Caesar was a Roman aristocrat from the old family of Iulii, which claimed lineage from Aeneas's son Anchises (Iulus). Caesar supported Marius's military control as well as Pompey's restoration of the tribunes. Ambitious and intelligent, he knew how to gain popularity. In 65 BC, in the role of aedile, he spent a lot of public (or Crassus's) wealth on public works and entertainments. In 63 BC he became Pontifex Maximus (the leading priest), by bribing his way to the function. In 62 BC he was mentioned as one of the conspirators, along with Catiline, against the state, but Cicero claimed this was impossible. In 61 BC, Caesar became the governor of Further Spain (present-day Portugal).

The First Triumvirate (60 BC)

The First Triumvirate (the rule of three) was an alliance formed by Pompey, Crassus, and Caesar, who thought they would be even more powerful together. All of them were unsatisfied in their ambitions – Pompey's request for land was blocked by the elite; his mates overshadowed Crassus, and Caesar was not allowed consideration for the consulship in absentia – and they had to do something about it.

Caesar was required to be in Rome in person so that he could be a candidate, so he returned, allied with Pompey and Crassus, and formed the First Triumvirate. Caesar was elected consul in 59 BC. The Senate could not decline the demands of the three generals so easily. Caesar helped Pompey get both the parcels for his soldiers and approval of his reimbursement at the end of the war in the east. Caesar married his daughter Julia to Pompey to fortify their friendship.

Caesar and the Gauls

Caesar became Proconsular Governor in Gaul, which was a position that brought him colossal power. He could still actively participate in Rome's political life, but he also had an army, a significant provincial command with an army, and the possibility of conquest. So, he conquered everything from Rome to the coastlines of the Atlantic and the North Sea. He even led expeditions to Britain, which was believed to be the end of the world.

Caesar himself wrote a detailed account of his nine-year campaign known as the Gallic War. His writing was biased without a doubt – it had to serve him marketing after all – but it contains fantastic detail of this war. Discipline, logistics, quarreling surrounded by the enemy, and the ruthless destruction of risings against Roman rule, he wrote about all of that. Caesar was brutal to the Gauls, to be a Roman hero.

Chapter 9 – Senatus Populus-Que Romanus (SPQR) and Its Downfall

While Caesar was busy fighting in Gaul and Britain and establishing himself as a true Roman Leader, back in Rome, there was a lot of tension. The tribune Publius Clodius Pulcher ("the Handsome") was in control, but his activities endorsed the private interests and competitions that were the trademark of Roman politics. He used Caesar's funds to pay gangs of hooligans to do what they were told. Clodius Pulcher also banished Cicero from Rome using questionable legality of the killings after the supporters. Then he overthrew the king of Cyprus, so he could use his fortune. Next, he imprisoned Pompey in his own home. Pompey reacted with similar measures, employed gangsters, and managed to pass a law which allowed Cicero to return. Pulcher even tried to seduce Caesar's wife, Pompeia. His lewd behavior justified Pompey to increase his authority in Rome at Caesar's expense.

The official name of the Republic at this point was SPQR, meaning the Senate and People of Rome. The title is ironical because the people of Rome had less power than ever before. The care of their interests was handed over to the tribunes, but a tribune could be - and often was - corrupted to his core.

The people of Rome (PQR in SPQR) was a political body made up of all male citizens (the women had no right to vote) of Rome – approximately a million of them in 63 BC. But most of them never turned up in the elections. On the other hand, no one could become a consul unless the people elected him.

Cicero against Catiline: The story that encapsulates 63 BC Rome

Lucius Sergius Catilina (or Catiline) was an angry, bankrupt noble. He was believed to be the architect of a plot to liquidate Rome's elected officials and burn the Senate to the ground. That way, he would write off the debts of rich and poor alike, and debts were again one of the significant problems of populace.

This was one of the central political events of the century. Caesar had some radical ideas about the best way to punish the conspirators. Crassus acted behind the scenes. But the main protagonist and Catalina's opponent was Marcus Tullius Cicero, the renowned orator, politician, philosopher, priest, poet, storyteller, and more. Cicero's name was on the list of those marked out for elimination. This fabulous orator never failed to use his verbal artistry to claim that he had exposed Catiline's awful plan and saved the state. The truth is that this was a turning point in his career, but his finest moment wasn't going to last, nor was the state that he claimed to have saved.

Cicero and Catilina, of course, disagreed politically but was more than the conflict of ideology. Even though they both were at the top of Roman politics, these two men came from different backgrounds. Catilina's family traced its ancestry back to the legendary founding fathers of Rome. They were said to have arrived before Rome even existed. Then there was his great-grandfather fought against Hannibal. Catiline himself was elected to many of junior political offices, but now he was dangerously close to bankruptcy. His name was linked to crimes such as the violent death of his first wife and child and sexual relationship with a "virgin" priestess. But his financial difficulties originated partly from his frequent attempts to buy his way into consulship. He had already been defeated in both 64 and 63 BC, and since the elections were a costly business, he ran out of wealth.

Cicero's story was entirely different. He was a "new man" like Marius. Cicero came from a small town, and no one in his family ever entered the Roman political arena. But he cultivated connections on the highest level and his talent that allowed him to speak his way to the top. He was a brilliant advocate, a superstar, and was elected to junior offices just as easily as Catilina. In 64 BC, Cicero won, Catiline lost. The votes of the wealthy always had more weight, and the Roman elite decided Cicero was a better choice. The second consul elected that year was Gaius Antonius Hybrida, uncle of Marcus Antonius.

In 63 BC, both Cicero and Catiline were candidates again. Cicero acted as he feared his life. He postponed the elections, and when they finally took place, he arrived with an armed guard. A military breastplate was noticeable under his toga. It turned out this tactic worked. Catiline's program worked for Cicero, too, as it further alienated the former patrician from the elite.

Shortly after the elections, Cicero started to receive more proofs of conspiracy from sources such as a certain Fulvia, the girlfriend of one of Catiline's 'collaborators.' Other proofs came with the help of Crassus's money, and Cicero avoided a true assassination attempt in November. Armed forces were grouping outside the city, and Cicero called for the senate to meet and formally condemn and banish Catiline. A decree that allowed Cicero emergency measures to "make sure that the state should come to no harm" had already been issued. Now the senate listened to Cicero's case against Catiline. As always, he was brilliant. His speech was a blend of anger, passion, humility and solid fact. He recapped Catiline's infamous past, expressed heartfelt regret that he had not responded to the threat quickly enough; and revealed details about the conspiracy. Catiline came in person to face the accusation and asked the senators not to trust everything they heard. All he had to say is to insult Cicero's modest background and compare it with his own. But his position was hopeless, and he had to leave the city.

Catiline joined his supporters who had made an army at the border of Rome. In the meantime, Cicero exposed those that were still inside the city. They were arrested, and they tried to act innocent. When the home of one of them was found filled with weapons, he claimed that weapon collecting was his hobby.[33]

Even though the senate took some time to discuss the destiny of the conspirators, there was never a proper trial. Cicero used his emergency authority, had them all executed, and announced their death in a single word: *vixere*. Literally, it means "they have lived" (but now they are dead).

A few weeks later, Roman legions overpowered Catiline's army in Northen Italy. Catiline fell fighting heroically as a true leader, but the Roman commander, Antonius Hybrida, found an excuse to miss the final battle. Maybe he secretly supported Catiline, and all this hassle had something to do with Crassus. Also, no one knew for sure on which side was Caesar.

Cicero was celebrated as *pater patriae*, one of the finest titles one could have in a society such as Rome. But on his last day as consul, his rivals did not allow him to speak to the people. "Those who have punished others without a hearing ought not to have the right to be heard themselves,"[34] they said. In 58 BC, the people of Rome voted to banish anyone who had put a citizen to death without trial. Cicero immediately left Rome and spent a year in North Greece. Eventually, the people voted for him to return. His supporters welcomed him warmly, but his house was wiped out and a shrine to Libertas risen instead. He never managed to restore his political career.

Chapter 10 – The Rise and Fall of Julius Caesar and the End of the Roman Republic

The Roman Republic had been declining for years, but finally ended in 43 BC. 15 years later, Rome became the Roman Empire. A single man, Octavian Augustus, modified the regulation of the Republic in a way that he held absolute power.

Caesar versus Pompey

During the First Triumvirate, Crassus, Pompey, and Caesar, each backed by a personal army, forced the Senate to do whatever they required. By 53 BC Crassus was dead, and Caesar and Pompey became rivals – and were yet to become enemies. Both of them had imperium: the power to command an army.

In 50 BC the consul Gaius Marcellus requested Caesar's withdrawal from Gaul. Scribonius Curio, a bankrupt tribune whose support Caesar had bought, vetoed Marcellus's demand, so the consul pleaded Pompey to protect the Republic and use his army and make Caesar surrender his command. Caesar said he would give up his command if Pompey did the same, but this never happened. New governors were sent to the Gallic provinces. The new tribune, Marcus Antonius, tried to veto this decision but was warned he'd soon be dead if he did so. Cicero, even though he was against Caesar and the Triumvirate, wanted to discuss an amicable solution, but the Senate gave Pompey the Senatus Consultum Ultimum, and the power to make Caesar a public enemy and get rid of him once and for all.

Crossing the Rubicon

Caesar had two options available. He could surrender to Rome as a public enemy or stay there and be taken by his adversaries in Gaul. Then he chose the third option: in 49 BC, he took his army from Gaul, crossed the river Rubicon and attacked Italy. This could be a declaration of war against the Republic, but Caesar had nothing to lose. *Iacta alea est.*

Caesar was still willing to share power with Pompey, but the latter was not – or at least his advisors weren't. The war started, Caesar won, and Pompey escaped to Greece.

Caesar seized his city. The senators were frightened, but Caesar's troops were highly disciplined. They didn't ruin anything and did not kill Caesar's opponents. Caesar's reputation was kept intact. Moreover, he made many popular gestures – canceled debts, brought Italians into the Senate, and allowed the men who had been exiled by Sulla and Pompey to return to Rome. Even Pompey's soldiers who remained in Rome were spared and recruited under Caesar.

Caesar sent an army led by Scribonius Curio to Africa, to deal with the rebellion by the governor Attius Varus, who supported Pompey. Curio was defeated. But Caesar almost at the same time went to Pompey's province of Spain and defeated Pompey's two deputies in a month.

Meanwhile, Pompey gathered a vast army in Greece, which included Roman soldiers from border garrisons. He had two times more men than Caesar. Pompey intended to retake Italy, but that didn't work out. The two armies met several times, and Caesar finally beat Pompey at the Battle of Pharsalus in 48 BC. Most of the enemy forces were captured, but Caesar ordered his men to 'spare your fellow citizens.' Pompey escaped to Egypt where he was murdered by the men of the boy-king Ptolemy XIII. When Caesar came for him, he was given his dislodged head. Caesar was angry with Pompey's murders and got them executed.

Ptolemy XIII hoped Caesar would support him against his sister Cleopatra VII. Instead, Caesar placed her to throne by supporting her other brother and husband, Ptolemy XIV. Meanwhile, Cleopatra became his lover and gave birth to his son.

A Romantic Digression: Caesar and Cleopatra

The Egyptian episode deserves a closer look. Some events – not only crucial for the history of the ancient world, but also vital for Caesar's life and career – happened during this visit.

Ptolemy XIII, the ruler of Egypt, depended on Rome's support, maybe even more than other Roman allies at the time. He had no public support whatsoever. His sister and wife (strange as it sounds, but the Egyptian rulers, especially the Ptolemies, loved to keep the power within the family) was the famous Cleopatra VII. She was older and smarter than her brother/husband. People loved her for her generosity and the fact that she was the only person in this ruling dynasty who actually cared about them and spoke Egyptian. She became a queen when she married the legitimate heir to the throne, the aforementioned Ptolemy XIII. He was still a boy at the time – something that enabled Cleopatra to rule alone – but eventually he grew up. He was an entirely different kind of a ruler than she was. Ptolemy XIII was cruel, arrogant, and actually very weak. The people of Egypt hated him, and supported Cleopatra. The ruling couple turned into two of the greatest enemies in the war for the throne of Egypt.

Ptolemy used some dishonest methods to turn the people of Egypt against their beloved queen. His supporters falsified and distributed a decree in her name that all supplies of grain should be sent to Alexandria rather than to the rest of Egypt. As a result, Cleopatra had to abandon the country and find shelter in Syria. But she didn't leave for good. In 48 BC, she gathered an army and came to the border of Egypt, determined to replace Ptolemy on the throne. This was when Caesar stepped in.

Caesar had two reasons to come to Alexandria. He pursued Pompey, but he had also been invited to mediate between Ptolemy and Cleopatra. Ptolemy sent him Pompey's head – an act with vague meaning that could be seen as either a proof of amity or a threat. Caesar was shocked. Pompey was his rival, but Caesar believed he had not deserved such a horrible death. Enraged, Caesar marched into Alexandria and took control over the palace. He ordered both sides to discharge their armies and meet him. Cleopatra knew her husband wouldn't let her enter the city alive. So she entered in disguise, hidden inside an oriental rug, which was delivered to Caesar as a present. Caesar fell in love immediately and that night he and Cleopatra became lovers.

Ptolemy, on the other side, felt betrayed. But he was history. After six months, he was found drowned in the Nile. Cleopatra was almost ready to take the throne. But, as a woman, she was not a legitimate heir. Luckily, her even younger brother Ptolemy XIV was, so she married him. The new Ptolemy was too young for marriage consumption. That pleasure belonged to Caesar. Cleopatra gave birth to his son named Ptolemy Caesar, also known as Caesarion.

Their romantic relationship lasted until Caesar's death. She spent two years in his palace, and was given a number of gifts and titles. After he was murdered, she went back to Egypt, arranged the murder of her husband, and married her son, Caesarion, to make sure he would end up on the throne. That, unfortunately, never happened. After the next episode in her love life – the one that involves Mark Anthony – Octavian Augustus had the young Caesarion executed.

Triumph at Rome

On the way back to Rome in 47 BC, Caesar defeated all opponents from Pharnaces in five days. His victory was summed up in the famous words: *Veni, vidi, vici* (I came, I saw, I conquered). In 46 BC he won the Battle of Thapsus against an army loyal to Pompey.

Caesar became the sole leader of the Roman world. The Senate made Caesar Dictator for ten years. He had to repair the damage, restore the Republic, settle veterans, and reestablish law and order. Caesar brought in concrete solutions to reinstate stability in the Roman world. His reforms included:

- Sparing Pompey's supporters if they were willing to come over to Caesar.
- Reducing the number of idle troublemakers by halving the number of Romans who depended on the free corn dole.
- Settling his army veterans in foreign colonies.
- Setting up new colonies and giving them Roman or at least Latin status.
- Granting Roman citizenship to those who deserved it.
- Permitting Italians, and some Gauls, to the Senate, and extending the Senate's awareness of issues outside Rome.
- Upgrading road links to the port at Ostia.
- Granting Latin status to Transpadane Gaul.
- Reducing taxes in some provinces.

Caesar was admired for his reforms. He indeed had done a lot to assure stability in the Roman world. The Senate thought Caesar would operate within the Republican system, but this wasn't the case. He still had his powerful army. Moreover, he appointed himself a consul several years and took over the powers of a tribune. Traditionalists criticized him for suppressing the Republican system. He filled the Senate with his men and did whatever he wanted. His word was law. Caesar crossed the line several times, and one of his mistakes was that he allowed statues of himself along with those of gods and the kings. His coins had his portrait. Everything he did annoyed his quiet opponents. In 44 BC, Caesar became Dictator Perpetuus (Dictator for Life) and acted like a king.

The Roman people only cared about stability and leadership; they were happy because Caesar's reforms put an end to the years of struggle. But senators resented him, and Cicero called him a tyrant. Caesar thought he was invincible and did not have a bodyguard anymore. He was preparing to defeat Parthia, fulfill a prophecy and become a Roman king.

Caesar's adversaries knew he would leave on 18 March 44 BC if they didn't do something immediately. On March 15, 44 BC, the Ides of Brutus and Cassius stabbed him at a Senate meeting. They thought they had liberated Rome from a tyrant and would be celebrated as the liberators of the Republic, but they were wrong. Brutus and other conspirators found the empty Forum. The senators left, and so did everybody else. The conspirators knew they should leave the town.

Mark Antony took charge. He was Caesar's co-consul and loyal supporter over many years. Cicero – who was one of the conspirators - believed Antony should have been eliminated too.

Caesar's funeral triggered public rage. The crowd vandalized the Forum and lynched someone who looked like one of the conspirators. A group of men hurried toward Brutus' and Cassius's homes to kill them, but they had escaped and fled Rome.

Mark Antony or Octavian

Mark Antony managed to calm people and stabilize a possibly catastrophic situation after Caesar's assassination. He intentionally let the conspirators to get away, gave some land away from Rome to Caesar's veterans, and ended the dictatorship. Brutus and Cassius even became governors of provinces. But the Senate did not approve of the way Antony was spending funds and selling benefits using bogus documents. Finally, the Senate named someone else as Caesar's heir – his great-nephew and adopted son, Gaius Octavius Thurinus, who became known as Octavianus. Octavian was a legitimate heir, according to Caesar's will.

The End of the Republic (44–43 BC)

The 18-year-old Octavian promptly arrived from Epirus, where he attended military training, to Rome, changing his name to Gaius Julius Caesar Octavianus, to make sure he would win over Caesar's troops. The tension between himself and Marc Antony, who was carelessly spending Caesar's fortune, started right away. Cicero also criticized Antony for his opportunism.

Antony became governor in Gaul and intended to move the army from Macedonia into Gaul. He was planning to attack Brutus, and the Senate declared him a public enemy.

The Senate wanted Octavian to become an ally of Brutus and punished him by holding up the money when they didn't want to do so. At last, Octavian met Antony, and together with Marcus Aemilius Lepidus, the Governor of Spain, they formed the Second Triumvirate, which lasted for five years. The power of the Second Triumvirate diminished the one of the Senate. Octavian,

Antony, and Lepidus could do whatever they wanted. The law that established the Second Triumvirate was passed on 27 November 43 BC. It was the end of the Roman Republic. Just a decade later, Octavian would become the undisputed master of the Roman Empire.

Conclusion

The rise and decline of the Roman Republic have a distinctive place in the history of the Western world. From modest beginnings on seven hills alongside the River Tiber, the city of Rome became the dominant power in the ancient Mediterranean world. Led by the senatorial nobles, Republican military forces triumphed over Carthage and the successor monarchies to Alexander the Great and took the nearby cities and tribes to east and west under Roman rule. However, the accomplishment of the Republic was also a seed of catastrophe. The same forces that propelled the growth and conquests of Rome, and the treasures that conquests brought, caused political, social, and economic crisis and rushed the Republic into the chaos of civil war. The Senate and other Republican institutions couldn't cope with the weights of sustaining Rome's empire, and at the end, all power came into the hands of Octavianus Augustus, the first Roman emperor.

For the generations yet to come, the Roman Republic has offered a pattern, inspiration, and a warning. The legends of the Roman past and the heroes and enemies of the Republic have never stopped rousing the imagination. Books, films, and series still rely on that legacy today, even though their level of historical accuracy is far from perfect. The Republic's history itself is as fascinating as any fiction. It consists of moments of highest drama, from the mythical story of Romulus, Hannibal's journey over the Alps to Julius Caesar on the shores of the Rubicon and in the Senate on the Ides of March.

Two thousand years have passed since the Roman Republic fell, but its legacy is still alive. The Roman Empire which arose from the ashes of the Republic continued to rely on Republican traditions, even as imperial tyranny took the place of joint senatorial rule. The slow transformation of the Empire to Christianity added a new element, with admiration for Rome's antiquity combined with criticism of its pagan past.

Over the next couple of centuries, the influence of the Roman Republic faded, until the Renaissance. The political theory of Machiavelli and Shakespeare's plays helped revive the ideals, heroes, and anti-heroes of Republican history. This new awareness of the Roman past had more significant consequences in the 18th century when the great revolutions in France and America found inspiration in the notions of a Republican utopia. The Roman Republic still spreads through modern Western culture from politics to popular culture, influencing our lives so many ways.

Timeline[35]

All dates are B.C.

754/3 Traditional date of Rome's foundation

509 Expulsion of the Etruscan kings; the foundation of the Republic

494 First tribunes of the plebs elected

451/450 Law of the Twelve Tables

396 Capture of Veii

390/386 Gauls sack Rome

367 Licinio-Sextian laws: sharing of political power between the patricians and plebeians

282–275 War with Pyrrhus, king of Epirus

264 First gladiatorial combat in Rome

264-241 First Punic War

241 Sicily becomes the first Roman province

238 Provinces of Sardinia and Corsica established

225 Gauls invade Italy

219/218 Lex Claudia limits commercial activities of senators

218–201 Second Punic War

200–146 Wars against Macedonia and in the East

197 Two Spanish provinces established; Philip V, king of Macedonia, defeated at Cynoscephalae

196 Flamininus proclaims Greece's freedom 190 Antiochus III, king of Syria, defeated at Magnesia

186 Suppression of the Bacchanalian cult in Italy

168 Perseus, king of Macedonia, defeated at Pydna

149 First permanent jury court established

149-146 Third Punic War

146 Destruction of Corinth and Carthage; provinces of Macedonia and Africa established

133 Pergamum bequeathed to Rome by its last king, Attalus III

133–12 Reforms of the Gracchi brothers

129 Province of Asia established

121 Province of Gallia Narbonensis (Provence) established; first suspension of the constitution

112–105 War with Jugurtha, king of Numidia

107 Marius' army reforms

100 Province of Cilicia established

91–87 Social War: all Italians become Roman citizens; Sulla captures Rome

83–82 Civil war

82 Sulla captures Rome

82–79 Sulla controls Rome: restoration of the Republic

75/74 Province of Cyrenaica established

67 Province of Crete established; defeat of pirates

66–63 Pompey in the East

64 Province of Syria established 63 Province of Bithynia and Pontus established; consulship of Cicero; Catilinarian conspiracy

60 Political alliance of Pompey, Caesar, and Crassus

59 Province of Cyprus and province of IUyricum established; consulship of Caesar

58-50 Gallic War 49 Caesar crosses the Rubicon and invades Italy

49–45 Civil war between Caesar and his senatorial opponents (esp. Pompey and Cato)

44 Caesar is named dictator for life; Caesar is assassinated on the Ides of March

43 Triumvirate consisting of Antony, Octavian, and Lepidus; the assassination of Cicero

42 Brutus and Cassius die after defeat at Philippi

31 Battle of Actium: Octavian defeats Antony and Cleopatra

27 Octavian "restores the Republic" and takes the name Augustus

Part 2: The Roman Empire

A Captivating Guide to the Rise and Fall of the Roman Empire Including Stories of Roman Emperors Such as Augustus Octavian, Trajan, and Claudius

Introduction

The Roman Empire was one of the most powerful forces the world has ever seen.

But this isn't just the story of conquest or the incredible system of institutions that made it possible. The Roman Empire is not yet another boring historical topic. On the contrary, it wakes our imagination, scares us, and entertains us. This is the story of the fascinating men and women—the emperors, their wives, parents, brothers, sisters, and children—who gave the empire its characteristic charm. Some of them, like Marcus Aurelius and Antoninus Pius, were virtuous and wise; others—like Caligula, Commodus, and Caracalla—were monstrous, insane predators whose thirst for blood and sexual habits were beyond believable. We know so much about them because ancient historians such as Suetonius, Cassius Dio, and Pliny kept a very detailed record of the everyday life and habits of these imperial superstars. Not all of the stories are true—after all, the Romans were those who invented and developed political propaganda and information spinning—but they are nevertheless fascinating.

The story begins with the assassination of Julius Caesar, the end of the Roman Republic, the rivalry between Octavian and Antony, and its aftermath. It ends five centuries later when the empire collapsed under the pressures from within and outside its borders. The years in between were full of incredible events, curious deaths, awkward marriages, and deified tyrants. One thing is for sure, no matter whether you're a spoiled patrician kid or an ambitious military general, it was never easy to be the emperor of Rome.

At its peak under Trajan, in the 2nd century AD, Roman population consisted of nearly 100 million people who lived in a vast area of 5 million square kilometers—from Hadrian's Wall in northern England (and for a brief period Scotland) to the riverside of the Euphrates in Syria and the Sahara desert, and from Portugal to Persia (present-day Iran). It covered the entirety of Europe, completely surrounding the Mediterranean Sea (or as the Romans called it, "mare nostrum," meaning "our sea"), and parts of Africa and Asia. Eventually, it had become too large to defend itself. Its last rulers and the elite were too busy fighting each other. This is the story of the most important people and events between the two crucial events - the rise of Augustus in the first century BC and the final sack of Rome in the late fifth century AD.

Chapter 1 – From the Republic to the Empire: The Rise of Octavian

The Collapse of the Republic

The constitution of the Roman Republic was slowly rotting from the inside for decades. The official name of the state—SPQR (Senatus Populusque Romanus/the Senate and People of Rome)—meant less now than ever before. The first century BC - the final century of the Republic - was marked by powerful individuals rather than the ordinary citizens of Rome or even the Senate. From Marius and Sula to Pompey and Caesar, these influential men slowly and inevitably diminished the power of the institutions that had been built for centuries. They were in charge of their own private armies, strong enough to attack each other or even Rome itself. At the same time, they kept their rivals close and were married to each other's sisters and daughters.

Political intrigue and social unrest made the last years of the Roman Republic chaotic. The most powerful force of the ancient world nearly fell to pieces during a series of civil conflicts and bloodshed. The first warlords, generals Gaius Marius and Lucius Cornelius Sula, were the first to do serious damage to the authority of the Senate. The protagonists of the First Triumvirate, Marcus Licinius Crassus, Gnaeus Pompeius Magnus, and Gaius Julius Caesar, went even further. After Crassus' death, Pompey and Caesar went from being close friends, allies, and even family to rivals who fought for the control over the city of Rome and its provinces. Caesar won, but was murdered in 44 BC. The forming of the Second Triumvirate was the ultimate defeat for the Senate and the Republic. The new blend of alliance and rivalry emerged between Caesar's loyal supporter, Marcus Antonius (Mark Antony), and the new guy in the story, Gaius Julius Caesar Octavianus, remembered in history as Augustus.

The Death of Julius Caesar and Its Consequences

Caesar's greatest sin, according to those who murdered him, was that he tolerated, if not enjoyed, being seen and presented as a king of Rome. His statue stood in line with those of the ancient kings, his face was engraved on the coins, and his word was the last in the Senate. "I am Caesar, not Rex"[36], he used to say, probably with a subtle hint of irony. It didn't save him. The so-called "Liberators" wanted to set the Republic free from the autocrat, and so they did. But their act of killing Caesar was one of desperation. The elite that used to pull the strings in Rome were now in jeopardy. Brutus and the other Liberators had no public support and were compelled to leave Rome overnight or face the rage of the masses. They had chosen the former and disappeared, albeit for a short while only.

Meanwhile, Mark Antony took charge. He was one of Caesar's most loyal men from the very beginning. Antony defended Caesar's interests as tribune back in 49 BC, and also led parts of Caesar's army on a few occasions. In 44 BC, when the sinister Ides of March took place, he was Caesar's colleague in the consulship. He organized a public funeral for Caesar and channeled the fury of the people who flooded the streets of Rome. But, he also amnestied the conspirators and allowed them to escape alive, giving them the control over the provinces at the Eastern part of the Empire (the East from now on). This delicate situation did not escalate into a catastrophe, as Antony managed to keep everyone happy. Well, almost everyone. The Senate wasn't really supporting him, and as for Caesar's will, he had already named an heir. And it wasn't Antony.

Octavian, Antony, and the Second Triumvirate

The news found young Gaius Octavius Thurinus[37] in Northern Greece where he had enrolled in military training. Upon hearing what happened, he quickly returned to Rome to claim his inheritance, changing his name to Gaius Julius Caesar Octavianus (which he later enhanced more with various titles to indicate his "divine" origin, and even rebranded himself under the name of Augustus to take the blood off his hands[38], but let's not rush).

Octavianus Augustus.[39]
https://commons.wikimedia.org/wiki/File:Augustus_Bevilacqua_Glyptothek_Munich_317_cropped.jpg

Octavian (how we shall call him from now on) wasn't thrilled when he found out that Mark Antony had been carelessly spending available public funds and Caesar's private treasure in order to make everyone happy and buy his way onto the top. The two men had instantly become enemies. Former Caesar (and now Antony's) opponents around the Senate saw their chance. Cicero quickly added fuel to the fire. In his "Philippics,"[40] he said Antony was an opportunist with ambitions as criminal as Caesar's, but without any of Caesar's abilities. Antony did, according to Cicero, abandon dictatorship, but he ran monstrous marketing to protect himself and his criminal allies against honorable men.[41] The political situation in Rome was tense. Antony believed Octavian was planning to eliminate him and so he made sure to become the governor in Gaul with the idea of moving the army from Macedonia into Gaul.

At this point, Octavian lacked the ability to legitimately run an army since he was still a "privatus," a private citizen without any public or military office. However, he gained huge support among Caesar's men, thanks to the substantial funds he gathered for them. He did not have access to either public funds or Caesar's treasure (that is, what had been left of it, considering Antony's habits). Octavian was forced to make a great effort to find some money for the army, but it paid off. Octavian also had some support from the Senate and the elite who needed him to get rid of Antony and bring the Liberators back to Rome. So, they allowed him to lead the army against Antony.

In 43 BC, the Battle of Mutina took place. It was politically intricate, but in short, Antony wanted to attack Brutus; Octavian was after Antony, but he did not want to defend Brutus. Octavian won the battle, but Antony managed to escape. Since Octavian refused to join Brutus, the Senate made it hard for him to keep the troops on his side by holding back money. Octavian was left with little choice, and in August 43 BC, Octavian and his eight legions marched into Rome and took charge. Octavian made himself a consul and issued the so-called *Lex Pedia*, which sentenced all of the conspirators against Caesar.

But Octavian knew he wasn't done with the conspirators yet. So, in November the same year, he and Marcus Lepidus—the man who ran the temporary administration of Rome and was formerly one of Caesar's staff officers—met Antony near Bononia[42]. The three men agreed to establish "Triumviri Rei Publicae Constituendae" or The Second Triumvirate, which had the mission of restoring the republic as well as punishing all those who had something to do with Caesar's death. The Second Triumvirate became official on November 27th 43 BC. Its establishment diminished the power of the Senate altogether, since the three rulers (the aforementioned triumviri) could now appoint the magistrate and had the authority to decide to go to war whenever they wanted without asking anyone. The official name of the state, as well as of the triumvirate itself, included the word "Republic," but the republic was now a past that would never return.

By the end of the year, all the conspirators were either dead or banished from Rome. Three hundred senators and two thousand equestrians (a wealthy class of people who were not of patrician origin, but earned both cash and influence during the period of late Republic) who supported the Liberators had been slaughtered. Cicero's blood fell on Antony's hands. Octavian wanted to spare the old politician, but his colleague in the Triumvirate couldn't forgive him all those Philippics.

Despite the differences, the three men jointly ruled Italy and shared the provinces. Octavian took Africa, Antony took Gaul, and Lepidus took Spain. The Eastern Mediterranean, as well as the Mediterranean islands, were still in control of their enemies, Brutus, Cassius, and Sextus Pompey.

In 42 BC, Antony and Octavian took an army and went to Greece, leaving Lepidus to run Italy in their absence. They overcame Cassius's and Brutus's troops at the Battle of Philippi, and both Liberators ended up committing suicide.

Allies or Enemies?

The Second Triumvirate wasn't meant to last. Upon returning to Rome, Octavian and Antony accused Lepidus of disloyalty (although he did not do anything wrong, his son Lepidus the Younger was involved in a conspiracy against Octavian), sent him to Africa, and shared his provinces. But they both had the ambition of taking it all, and they both were indeed powerful enough to do so. In 42 BC, Julius Caesar had officially become a god, and the Romans made a temple in his honor. Octavian, as his adopted son, was now considered the son of a god. But

Antony had some advantages too. The victory at the Battle of Philippi was solely his. He was the more skilled general and the military mastermind who did everything right. Octavian was present, but he was sick and mostly inefficient.

Now that this war was over, Octavian returned to Italy, and Antony went to the east to expand the empire. Perhaps Antony thought that nothing especially noteworthy would happen in his absence. If he did, he was wrong.

When Octavian returned from Philippi, he confiscated vast properties and gave the land to retiring soldiers, which eventually led to another civil war. Mark Antony's closest family, his wife Fulvia and his brother Lucius Antonius, presented the opposition and most serious threat to Octavian. They assembled the dispossessed landowners, promising that all the land would be returned and the republic restored when Antony returned from the east. Empowered by rage and a mixture of self-interest and idealism, they even took control over the city of Rome, but their five minutes did not last. Octavian fought back, and they had to retreat to Perusia (present-day Perugia). They were under siege until 40 BC when they surrendered, but the civil war lasted for another decade, fostered by various parties that claimed to represent Caesar's legacy.

40 BC was also the year when Antony returned to Italy and provisionally sorted everything out. He wasn't welcome at first though. Octavian's forces refused to let him in, and he responded by taking the port of Brundisium. Eventually, the three triumvirs made a deal and decided to rule together for another five years. Fulvia was now history, so Antony married Octavian's sister, Octavia, to strengthen the bonds with his ally. But the situation was not as nice and simple as it may look now. To get a full understanding of these relationships, we need to have a look at what exactly Antony did in the east.

Antony's Mission and the Ever-Charming Cleopatra

Before the unfortunate Ides of March, Caesar had been planning to invade Parthia and retake Roman provinces such as Syria and Asia Minor. This became Antony's mission after Caesar's death. But he replaced Caesar in another way too, for there was someone that used to be Caesar's that was now Antony's.

Cleopatra was still in Rome during Caesar's death, but she promptly escaped to avoid the destiny of her lover. During the years that followed, she kept connections with several influential Romans, including Cicero's former son-in-law Dolabella. It didn't last, as this man did not live long. But then Antony appeared. This began the relationship that defined both of them and became one of the greatest love stories in the history of the west.

Cleopatra and Antony had already met years ago. She was only 15, and he was a part of an official delegation that met with her father. So, in 42 BC, Cleopatra was 28 ("the very time when women have the most brilliant beauty and are at the acme of intellectual power"[43]), and Antony was slightly over 40.

Antony actually went to Egypt to interrogate Cleopatra for financing Cassius, an enemy of Rome. (Despite her love story with Julius Caesar, this powerful woman kept finding ways to influence the political situation in Rome and its provinces. This sometimes included relations with Caesar's murderers.) She probably wouldn't have ended up well if she wasn't so irresistible, but she was and was fully aware of her power. Here is how Plutarch described her in the early second century AD:

"For her beauty, as we are told, was in itself not altogether incomparable, nor such as to strike those who saw her; but converse with her had an irresistible charm, and her presence, combined with the persuasiveness of her discourse and the character which was somehow diffused about her behavior towards others, had something stimulating about it. There was sweetness also in the tones of her voice; and her tongue, like an instrument of many strings, she could readily turn to whatever language she pleased [...]"[44]

Antony and Cleopatra enjoyed their affair, "an association called The Inimitable Lovers, and every day they feasted one another, making their expenditures of incredible profusion,"[45] while Antony's wife Fulvia opposed Octavian in a civil war that was bursting in Rome. When he finally heard the news from Rome, he remembered why he came to the east in the first place. He quickly prepared and went for Parthia (although it may look puzzling why he didn't go to Rome instead).

On the way, he received more news and learned that all the mess in Rome was Fulvia's fault, as she was desperately trying to take her husband from Cleopatra's embrace and make him come home. It was in 40 BC—when Fulvia had already lost her war, left Rome, traveled to meet Antony, and died on the way—that Antony decided to visit Rome. He took the opportunity to reconcile with Octavian, and the two men split the empire among themselves. The territories west of the Ionian Sea belonged to Octavian, and the east to Antony. Lepidus was no longer their equal, but they let him have Africa. Antony married Octavia. In 37 BC, however, he returned to Egypt, and a year later he married his true love, completely ignoring the existence of his Roman wife.

Antony and Cleopatra had three children. She also had a son with Julius Caesar, whom Octavian saw as a major threat since he could be a legitimate heir to the Roman Empire. In 34 BC, Antony handed his children incredible titles and the power over Armenia, Cyrenaica, Crete, and Syria. Octavian was truly upset by Antonius's actions and to deal with his Antony and Cleopatra problem by taking the Roman Empire in its entirety.

The final offense that served as justification for Octavian to attack Antony was made when Octavia went to see her husband in Athens, bringing gifts, treasures, and clothes for Antony's soldiers. According to Plutarch, she was "treated with scorn."[46] When she returned to Rome, Antony's men even expelled her from his house. As for Octavian, this was a clear sign that he and Antony would never be allies again.

The Battle of Actium and the End of Antony and Cleopatra

In 31 BC, Octavian fought Antony's and Cleopatra's armies in a sea battle off the coast of Actium (northern Greece). Antony was the more competent soldier, but numerous fights weakened his once magnificent army during his expedition in Parthia. Octavian, on the other hand, was well prepared for the battle. With Antony's and Cleopatra's armies clearly losing, Cleopatra escaped the battle with Antony following her, leaving many of his men behind. The Romans on both sides were certain that Marc Antony was enslaved by his affection of Cleopatra. In their eyes, he had lost all integrity.

When Octavian entered Alexandria in 30 BC, Antony's men, as well as numerous vassal kings of the eastern provinces, changed sides and joined him, leaving their former general alone. At the same time, Cleopatra locked herself in her tomb and sent servants to deliver the message to Antony saying that she was dead. Antony tried to stab himself to death, but did it clumsily. He remained alive, but with a fatal wound. In his last moments, he learned Cleopatra was actually alive and was taken to her, dying in her arms.

Meanwhile, Octavian took charge of Cleopatra's palace. He planned to take the queen to Rome and drag her through the streets in chains. But the Romans couldn't find a way to enter her tomb. Cleopatra negotiated with Octavian through the closed door, demanding that her kingdom be left to her children. During the negotiations, Octavian's men raised ladders and entered the tomb through the window. The queen of Egypt attempted to stab herself, but was quickly disarmed and imprisoned, just like her children. After Antony's funeral, Cleopatra arranged for a basket of figs with a hidden venomous snake to be taken to her. After her death, Octavian quickly got rid of young Caesarion, the son of Cleopatra and Julius Caesar.

From that point onwards, Egypt, as well as the entire Roman Empire, belonged to Octavian.

Chapter 2 – The Age of Augustus

The Princeps Augustus

It has been debated for centuries when exactly the Roman Empire started. Was it in the moment of forming the Second Triumvirate or after the battle of Actium? Was Augustus (Octavian) the first emperor or was that Julius Caesar? The famous Roman historian Suetonius[47] wrote about The Twelve Caesars: Julius Caesar and the first 11 emperors of Rome, from Augustus to Domitian. Plutarch actually referred to Octavian as Caesar.[48]

Be that as it may, in 27 BC Octavian became Imperator Caesar Divi Filius Augustus—the holy (Augustus) son of god (Divi Filius) Caesar. His change of name was profound. Octavian belonged to the past. Augustus was a revered one, the high priest (Pontifex Maximus), and at the same time, often presented as a heroic warrior of semi-divine origin. With his rise to power, the period in Roman history known as the Principate had begun, which would last until the end of the Crisis of the Third Century in 284 AD.

This era is characterized by the rule of a single emperor (princeps), but also by an attempt to maintain the illusion of the formal continuity with the Roman Republic. This was very important because no Roman ever wanted to reintroduce a legal monarchy and we've already seen that an accusation of wanting to be a Rex could easily be turned into a death sentence.

Paradoxically as it may seem, Augustus was careful to not accept the title of a monarch or Rex even though he was more powerful and had some real monarchs as vassals. Officially, he was a princeps, first among equals, but that was merely a façade. The Roman historian Tacitus wrote that Augustus "laid aside the title of triumvir and paraded himself as consul and as content with the tribunician authority for looking after the commons. The soldiery he enticed with gifts, the people with corn, and all alike with the charms of peace and quiet; and thus he edged forward bit by bit (itnsurgere paulatim), taking into his hands the functions of Senate, magistrates, laws."[49] In fact, it wasn't quite new that senators, who were supposed to be elected, continuously came from a limited number of aristocratic families. These men formally held all the important functions within government and agreed with everything Augustus said.

Senators were supposed to be elected, but they always came from the same aristocratic families. Senators also held all the most important government jobs. In theory, the Senate was a kind of parliament. In practice, all it did was agree to the Emperor's laws.

Provinces safely within the Roman Empire were run by a governor, who was usually a senator. However, provinces on the Empire's borders, such as Britain where the legions (military formations consisting of ten cohorts, each of five or six centuries) were stationed and the wars took place, were always run by an army general.

Augustus of Prima Porta.[50]
https://commons.wikimedia.org/wiki/File:Statue-Augustus.jpg

How He Did It

From our point of view, it looks like Augustus (or Octavian) was lucky and that it was easy for him to take all that power that he wanted to. But it was not. It was hard to make his war against Antony appear like a war against an outside enemy (Egypt and Cleopatra), rather than internal conflicts between the triumvirs. It was also hard to preserve the institutions of the republic and give up some privileges. And it was tremendously hard to sustain and control a large army that had never been used to being loyal to the state itself. But he somehow managed to do it and became one of the most powerful emperors that the world has ever seen.

Upon returning to Rome, Octavian had some tough decisions to make. For him to be accepted as someone who respects the tradition and institutions of Rome, he had to give up the command over the army. But if he really gave up the power over the army, that might have meant more civil war. Besides, why would he give up the power and influence he had rightfully earned? He managed to find a way to use the means of the republic to preserve his authority by restoring the Senate and giving them command over the army and other non-military affairs. But, Octavian got rid of the senators he deemed unsuitable and created a list of formal criteria for entry to the Senate, thus ensuring that he himself controlled the Senate.

Augustus as Pontifex Maximus.[51]
https://commons.wikimedia.org/wiki/File:Augustus_as_pontifex_maximus.jpg

Octavian also had some very powerful and loyal friends that he could count on. For example, the wealthy equestrian Gaius Maecenas not only fought together with Octavian, but also spent a fortune supporting his political career. He financed poets and writers as a patron and was solely responsible for the creations of literary jewels such as Aeneid, which praised Octavian's ancestry as well as his rule. Another important person in Octavian's life was Marcus Vipsanius Agrippa. Agrippa was a highly capable soldier and tactician who made Octavian's military successes possible. He married Octavian's daughter, Julia. Maecenas and Agrippa jointly managed internal affairs in Rome, but Agrippa also took charge of the east and Gaul.

Equally important in Augustus' life was Livia, his second wife. It is interesting that both Augustus and Livia were already married, but it didn't stop them. Augustus divorced Scribonnia, the mother of Julia, his only child, in 39 BC and married Livia in 38 BC. Livia was married to Tiberius Claudius Nero, who was Augustus' political opponent and a supporter of Pompey, before divorcing him and marrying Augustus. The couple had no children. The princeps adopted Livia's (and her ex-husband's) sons Tiberius and Drusus, and eventually made Tiberius his heir.

The Augustan Legacy

The deep paradox between the figure of Augustus, the powerful Caesar, and the one of the humble princeps who restored the Republic is best illustrated in a recently discovered coin from 28 BC. One side of the coin depicts young Caesar Octavian with a laurel and the inscription "Imperator Caesar, son of the Divine, Consul for the sixth time." The other side of the same coin displays Octavian sitting on a magistrate's bench, wearing a civilian toga. The caption on that side says, "He revived the rights and laws of the Roman People."[52]

Augustus initiated a massive reconstruction of Rome, along with social reform. He finished the construction of Julius Caesar's projects such as the Temple of Venus Genetrix, the goddess marked as the divine ancestress of the family of Iulii, to which he and Julius Cesar belonged. At the same time, he consistently played his role as a defender of the republic. Augustus was also always making sure to make his personal rivals look like the enemies of the Roman Republic. Brutus and Cassius, according to him, "waged war against the Republic," Sextus Pompey was a pirate, and Mark Antony headed a "faction that oppressed the Republic."[53] We should not forget that the term "Roman Empire" is a modern invention. The official name of the state was still SPQR and the institutions of the republic survived until the age of Domitian, albeit in the shadow of the emperor.

Beyond the border of Rome, he set up a standing army. His dynamic campaign of expansion had the purpose of making Rome safe from barbarians and securing the Augustan peace. There were some setbacks, such as the Pannonian revolt (AD 6-9) and the advancement of aggressive Germanic armies, so the expansion stopped for a certain period. However, the army kept protecting the "fortress Rome"[54] efficiently, ensuring the peace and prosperity within Rome itself.

The army was loyal to both Rome and Augustus. The Republic paid soldiers, but they received bonuses and awards from the imperial family. In the year 6 AD, Augustus founded the soldiers' treasury and contributed 170 million sesterces, which was an impressive amount. This Caesar, just like his predecessor Julius, knew how to make the people of Rome (and his soldiers in particular) happy.

The Golden Age of Latin Literature

Coins and statues were not enough for Augustus. He wanted his image to have a more profound effect and was well aware of the power of literature and poetry. So, he became a patron of leading Roman poets, such as Horace, Virgil, and Propertius. Another author whom Augustus supported generously was Livy, one of the most prominent Roman historians.

The Augustan Age was certainly one of the most admired periods, not only in Latin literary history, but also in the history of world literature. Ovid's *Metamorphoses* and Virgil's *Aeneid* are still best-sellers among classics. These works can be classified as committed or engaged literature, with the purpose of promoting the image of the ruler, but it would be wrong to see them merely as political pamphlets. Their literary value, depth and power, and polished, sophisticated form is simply striking even today.

Generally, these poems and narratives glorified civil peace and prosperity that marked the Augustan era. The most common themes include love, nature, and patriotism. And surprisingly, these poems are not dull. *Metamorphoses*, for example, comprise over 200 captivating—and sometimes disturbing—mythological stories in a chronological order, from the creation of world to the Augustan Age.

Tereus, Procne, and Furies - an engraving for a 16th-century edition of Metamorphoses. Tereus is married to Procne, but falls in love with her sister Philomela, whom he rapes, cutting off her tongue afterward so she wouldn't be able to speak about it. Procne reads the signs on the tapestry that Philomela made and figures out what happened. Infuriated, Procne takes ghastly revenge; she kills her and Tereus's only son, Itys, and cooks him for dinner. Tereus enjoys the meal, and at the end of it, his wife throws their son's disembodied head at him. They all end up turning into birds.[55]
https://commons.wikimedia.org/wiki/File:Virgil_Solis_-_Tereus_Philomela.jpg

    The *Aeneid* is an epic poem, equally famous as Metamorphoses, from the same period. Virgil follows the Homeric tradition and deals with the Trojan War and its consequences equally brilliantly, but he focuses on the Trojans rather than the Greeks by following the Trojan hero Aeneas. Virgil had spent nearly 12 years writing it and, disappointed by the outcome, almost burned it. It was the order from Caesar Augustus himself that saved the manuscript from the flames, with a reason more important than the emperor's love for poetry. The *Aeneid* is a story of how the Trojan prince Aeneas went to Italy and united his people with the Italians, creating the basis for the later city of Rome. According to the myth that every Roman knew, Aeneas's son Ascanius, or Iulus—the ascendant of Julius Caesar—founded Alba Longa. Furthermore, this epic highlights another myth: Aeneas was a descendant of the goddess Venus, and so were his children and all the *Iulii* Caesars. The *Aeneid* instantly became Rome's national epic and a direct endorsement of Augustus's rule after the long period of civil war.

Chapter 3 – The Julio-Claudian Dynasty After Augustus: From Tiberius to Nero

Rome in the first century AD was republican and monarchial at the same time. The institutions were growing stronger under Augustus that operated much like present-day democracy[56]. As for the monarchical part, Augustus wanted it to be hereditary, with the power kept within the dynasty to which Julius Caesar and himself belonged. But it wasn't easy for Augustus to find an heir, not only because he did not have a son, but because all the men that he had chosen to proceed with his legacy kept dying before him.

Augustus's first choice was Agrippa, his loyal friend and an extremely capable individual in both war and peace, experienced in governing multiple provinces. That's why Augustus' married his daughter, Julia, to Agrippa, to make him a part of the family. Agrippa would have most likely been a great emperor, but unfortunately he died too soon, during the conquest of the upper Danube River region. But Agrippa had two sons with Julia, Gaius and Lucius. Those boys were Augustus's real grandchildren and the most legitimate heirs that he could possibly have. Sadly, they too predeceased him. Both of them died of sudden illnesses. Augustus was forced to, albeit unwillingly, make his adopted sons Drusus and Tiberius the heirs to his position and power. Both of them, just in case someone died again. It was essential to have an option B because they were commanding large armies, were continuously sent on military campaigns, and could get killed at anytime. Then, during his return from a successful campaign, Drusus fell off his horse and died.

Another potential heir worth mentioning was Germanicus, another *Claudii* (the Claudii were the descendants of Tiberius Claudius Nero (not Nero the emperor but Roman praetor in 42 BC, the father of Tiberius and Drusus)) adopted into *Iulii*. His father was Drusus, and his mother was the daughter of Mark Antony and Octavia. As for Germanicus himself, he was a man of virtue, a renowned general, and the Roman equivalent of Alexander the Great.[57] Augustus was determined to make him the heir, but Livia supported Tiberius. Under the influence of his wife, Augustus agreed to make Tiberius his heir, but under one condition—Tiberius had to adopt Germanicus and make him his own heir.

"Great Cameo of France" – Roman artwork from the 1st century AD featuring several members of the Julio-Claudian dynasty.[58]
Cabinet des Médailles, CC BY-SA 3.0 <http://creativecommons.org/licenses/by-sa/3.0/>, via Wikimedia Commons
https://commons.wikimedia.org/wiki/File:Great_Cameo_of_France_CdM_Paris_Bab264_white_background.jpg

Augustus' dynasty was called Julio-Claudian because the following emperors descended from him and from his wife Livia's ex-husband Tiberius Claudius Nero. The first one, Tiberius, was born as an *Claudii* (he was the son of the eponymous Claudius), but was adopted into the *Iulii* while the rest of them had the Julian origin. They descended not from Augustus and his daughter, but from Julia, Julius Caesar's sister.

The Sorrowful Emperor and a Forbidden Love: Tiberius

Tiberius knew very well that he was an unloved stepson and an unwanted heir. In his first meeting with the Senate after Augustus' death, he rejected the fact that he had "succeeded to his father's station." The senators put a considerable amount of effort in trying to get him to acknowledge his supremacy.[59] He had no choice at that moment but to become an emperor and was actually a good one for a while.

Years before Augustus' death, Tiberius's military reputation was remarkable. He recovered parts of Roman provinces after disasters and proved himself as a great leader. Now that he had become an emperor (AD 14), he continued to lead Rome in the same direction as Augustus. The priorities remained the same: the reconstruction of the Roman Empire and keeping Rome safe within its borders. He had no intention of expanding the borders, but they were expanded; in AD 17, his nephew and adopted son, Germanicus, conquered Germania (hence Germanicus).

Tiberius was indeed a smart politician, just as he was a capable military leader. He took advantage of whatever large event took place within the Roman sphere of influence. When the kings of Commagene and Cappadocia (who were "the client kings" under protection of Rome) died, Tiberius named those kingdoms as new provinces. He demonstrated Rome's power by constructing roads and other public buildings. Tiberius also generously helped many cities of Asia after a horrible earthquake and made people remember it by issuing and sending the coins that celebrated his generosity.

Roman economy and financial strategy under Tiberius were different than before. He was a frugal emperor. Even though he sent money to provinces, let people off their depths, and even cut taxes, he saved a lot of Roman money. But these changes were unpopular because he stopped financing public entertainments.

Eventually, Tiberius completely lost any interest of running the empire and decided to retreat from power. But when he retired, he delegated the power to Sejanus, the prefect of the Praetorian Guard, rather than to the Senate. That did not end well. Sejanus was ambitious and had already poisoned Germanicus; he was even responsible for the murder of Tiberius's son, Drusus. Tiberius avenged his unfortunate successors spectacularly, but his later years were marked by paranoia, with many innocent people (including two of Germanicus' sons) being killed because they might have been traitors.

It may seem that Tiberius was ungrateful for his status of Caesar's heir. In reality, he was in many aspects a victim of Augustus' despotism. Augustus had a bad habit of arranging the private lives of people around him in order to align them with his political ambitions. We've already seen that Augustus demanded the divorce of Tiberius' parents so he could marry Livia, Tiberius' mother. We also know that Tiberius was forced to adopt Germanicus. But now that Tiberius had become a part of the family, he was forced by Augustus to divorce his loving wife, Vipsania Agrippina (Agrippa's daughter from a previous marriage), with whom he had been happily married for eight years. The couple had one son, called Drusus the Younger. According to Suetonius,[60] Vipsania was pregnant for the second time when they divorced, and the child did not survive. Tiberius was now to marry Octavian's daughter, Julia. According to various sources, this marriage was a disaster, partly because Julia was rather promiscuous at the time and had a habit of sneaking out at night. Suetonius claims that Tiberius never ceased to love his first wife and regretted the divorce. He noticed her once in a public place and followed her, crying and begging her for forgiveness. This was seen as scandalous behavior, and Augustus made sure they never met again.

The years passed and Vipsania remarried, giving birth to at least six sons to her new husband, Gaius Asinius Gallus. In AD 20, she died. Ten years later, the emperor Tiberius, now with a history of paranoia and abusing power, made her husband Gallus a public enemy. The unfortunate man died in prison.

Tiberius himself died an ugly death, and no one seemed to care. He was most likely poisoned and then suffocated in bed. The man who arranged the assassination was Germanicus' third son, Caligula.

A God Wanna-Be: Caligula

At first, Caligula (his real name was Gaius, but we remember him by his nickname) was perceived to be a virtuous man, just like his father, Germanicus. But he was very different than his father. It wasn't obvious from the start, because he reversed some of Tiberius's unpopular measures, allowed the people whom Tiberius had banished to come home, and brought costly public entertainments back. He did several other things right—revived elections, further reduced taxes, finished numerous buildings—but that wasn't hard because Tiberius saved and left more money in the public treasury than anyone before or after him.

Caligula, however, had neither a military reputation nor political experience. He came to power in AD 37, and within a year managed to spend all the money. Eventually he became a ruthless tyrant, declared himself a god, and even set up a cult to Caligula. A lot of senators were killed, foreign policy was almost ruined, and rebellions started in many provinces (most notably Mauretania and Judaea). Caligula had his mother, grandmother, and many cousins killed and had incestuous relationships with his sisters. A coin issued during his reign had Caligula's image on one side and his sisters on the other.

Left: Emp. Gaius (Caligula); right: his three sisters: Agrippina (as Securitas), Drusilla (as Concordia), and Julia (as Fortuna).[61] *Classical Numismatic Group, Inc.* http://www.cngcoins.com, *CC BY-SA 2.5* <https://creativecommons.org/licenses/by-sa/2.5>, *via Wikimedia Commons* https://commons.wikimedia.org/wiki/File:Caligula_sestertius_RIC_33_680999.jpg

This emperor loathed the people of Rome, and the feelings were mutual. In AD 41, he ended up being hacked to death during a public performance.

A Surprise Emperor: Claudius

Caligula had no plans of having an heir, actually killing everyone who looked like they would ever get an opportunity of claiming the throne. The only male relative that got spared was his uncle, Claudius, because he never seemed like a threat. Claudius had numerous physical handicaps—he stammered, dribbled, and had a limp—and was overall seen as the family idiot. This prevented him from gaining experience as an administrator or a soldier, but in these special circumstances, his handicaps saved his life.

The Senate had seen the end of Caligula as the end of the Principate and the chance of restoring the republic. But the generals of the Praetorian Guard had more power and a different idea. They found Claudius (50 years old at the time) literally hiding behind the curtain and asked him to become their emperor. He, of course, accepted.

An 1871 painting depicting Claudius hiding behind the curtain[62]
https://commons.wikimedia.org/wiki/File:A_Roman_Emperor_AD41_detail.jpg

Claudius was actually extraordinarily intelligent and, thanks to Augustus, highly educated. As a historian, he was well aware of the situation and knew he had to keep the military on his side. He rewarded the Praetorian Guard generously, and they remained loyal to him.

Emperor Claudius.[63]
https://commons.wikimedia.org/wiki/File:Claudius_(M.A.N._Madrid)_01.jpg

Claudius knew he had to gain some reputation as a leader and conqueror, so he dealt (rather efficiently) with the crises in Mauritania and Judea and ended up conquering Britain in AD 43.

In Rome, Claudius allowed leading Gauls to join the Senate and gave this institution more freedom, if not more power. The senators were encouraged to express their opinions even when they did not agree with imperial decisions. Furthermore, the grain supply was enhanced by building a large harbor at Ostia. The citizens of Rome kept receiving gifts - from material aid and privileges to establishing new public entertainments - from their emperor.

But this emperor was not perfect. His temper was unpredictable, and he was too fond of gladiator matches and other games. Suetonius recorded that, unlike other emperors after having watched a fight, Claudius would rise, praise the fighters, and act like the men from the crowd. [64]

Also, according to the Senate, his wives had way too much power. His third and fourth wife, Messalina and Agrippina, encouraged Claudius' fear of conspiracies and were responsible for numerous deaths of senators and equestrians. Messalina was the mother of Claudius' son, Britannicus, and was executed for bigamy in AD 48. Agrippina was Caligula's sister and the mother to Lucius (aka Nero). Lucius was her son from a previous marriage whom she wanted as the emperor of Rome. So, she got rid of her husband and his own son, Britannicus. It was AD 54, and Nero was almost 17.

Mother's High Hopes and an Epic Failure: Nero

Some historians described Nero as a crazy egomaniac whom the people of Rome hated so much that they celebrated when he died.[65] Others say that Nero was generous and that the people of Rome were loyal to him, but that the Senators and the elite were not.[66] But let's start from the beginning.

As the son of Caligula's sister, Agrippina, and the adopted son of Claudius, Nero was the last emperor from the Julio-Claudian dynasty—and the youngest one. He was only 17 when he ended up an emperor with the consent of the Praetorian Guard and his mother. At that point, he was mostly interested in art, painting, music, sports, and his own popularity. His mother, on the other hand, was interested in ruling the Roman Empire through her teenage son. Other people who influenced the views and decisions of the young emperor included his tutor, the famous stoic philosopher, Seneca, and the Praetorian prefect Sextus Afranius Burrus. During the first couple of years, the bureaucracy worked just the way it did under Claudius. Nero spent lavishly on public constructions and helped the poor, but he raised taxes, albeit unwillingly, which provoked the anger of many. There was a bit of expansion of the Roman Empire when one of the generals conquered Armenia. But, very soon things began to change and spiral out of control. Rebellions in Britain and other provinces started to spread like the plague, and it was all a reflection of

Nero's incompetence and arrogance. He had never really learned how to govern a large empire, and most of the time he didn't really care.

Nero, Antiquario del Palatino.[67]
https://commons.wikimedia.org/wiki/File:Nero_Palatino_Inv618.jpg

However, Nero decided he didn't need his mom to manage him. Her interference was not just annoying; Agrippina was so obsessed with power that she saw any interests her son had shown–just like any sign of his personal integrity and independence—as a threat. She wasn't happy about her boy being an artist, but the real hostility had begun once she learned that Nero had an affair with a slave girl. The frustrated mother then grew close to Nero's wife, Octavia, and continuously attempted to control Nero's life at home. Nero couldn't stand it anymore and expelled her. But it wasn't over. Nero decided to get rid of Octavia and live with his mistress, Poppaea. Agrippina tried her best to separate the lovers. Seneca even said Agrippina had planned to kill her son to avoid bad publicity, but she was the one who ended up being murdered, just like Octavia.

The most famous incident that occurred during the reign of Nero was the Great Fire of Rome (AD 64). It was a catastrophe. A large area of the city got burned, including fourteen Roman districts with many homes and public buildings, such as Aventine above the Circus Maximus and Palatine, succumbing to the flames.[68] Except Tacitus, who was "unsure,"[69] all ancient historians[70] blamed Nero for the fire. Ancient sources report that he sang, danced, and played violin. It looked like he indeed needed some clear space to build the so-called Domus Aurea, or Golden

House, with a gigantic statue of himself—the 30-meter-tall Colossus of Nero. So maybe he did set the fire or got lucky. However the fire started, this was an opportunity for the emperor to show generosity, organize repair, and distribute charity—which he did.

The back side of the coin displays Nero helping the unfortunate citizens of Rome.[71]
Classical Numismatic Group, Inc. http://www.cngcoins.com, CC BY-SA 3.0 <http://creativecommons.org/licenses/by-sa/3.0/>, via Wikimedia Commons https://commons.wikimedia.org/wiki/File:Nero_charity.jpg

To deal with the rumors that he was personally responsible for the fire, Nero blamed the Christians, who were ruthlessly persecuted afterward. The same went for anyone who looked like they might engage in any kind of plot against Nero. Criticism of any kind was strictly forbidden. Military generals and even benevolent philosophers were executed, except Seneca, who was ordered to kill himself instead.

With any perceived threats to his empire squashed, in AD 67 to 68, Nero was on vacation in Greece, the country which he declared free, and then won the Olympics, despite falling off his chariot. He was not only allowed to win any games he participated in; people were also forced to listen to his musical performance and no one was permitted to leave the theatre. At the same time, the grain ships that were to deliver corn to Rome got diverted and ended up in Greece, causing a famine in Rome.

Nero wasn't attentive to the signs of conspiracy at all times and had missed some, which later prove fatal. He also caused a rebellion by killing a number of powerful men. Others, including those who would remain loyal if loyalty was appreciated, decided to bring him down. Common soldiers were unhappy with Nero's reign too since he owed them a lot. They were sick, tired, and prone to mutiny. Several revolts broke out in the provinces, and eventually the Praetorian Guard joined one of the rebel generals. After the Senate declared Nero an enemy of Rome, Nero finally realized he was lost and panicked. The only people who remained loyal to him were a few servants, whose help he enlisted to guide him through the process of killing himself. One of them was ordered to show him by example, and another needed to help the emperor finish this undesirable task. He died crying, "What an artist dies in me!" ("Qualis artifex pereo!")[72] It was 9 June AD 68. Nero was the last emperor of the Juliu-Claudian dynasty.

Chapter 4 – Civil War and the Year of the Four Emperors (AD 68–69)

Nero did not have an heir, and there was no one left in the Julio-Claudian dynasty who could claim the status of the emperor of Rome. But many had dreamed of being one, and since the Julio-Claudians were gone, it had become clear that the new emperor could come from any powerful family from any city within the Empire. For the first time since the death of Mark Antony in 30 BC, a civil war broke out. During a single year, known as the Year of the Four Emperors, three emperors—Galba, Otho, and Vitellius—rose and fell. The fourth, Vespasian, remained for a decade and founded the Flavian dynasty.

Galba

When in early AD 68 the governor of Gallia Lugdunensis, Caius Julius Vindex, rebelled against Nero, his intent, along with other opponents of Nero, was to replace him with someone reputable and accountable, like Servius Sulpicius Galba. At the time, the 71-year-old Galba was the governor of Hispania. After Nero's suicide, the dominant leaders of the opposition, the Praetorian Guard and the Senate, recognized Galba as Nero's successor.

What most ambitious leaders loved about Galba was the fact that he was considerably old and ill. He would die soon, and without an heir, and in the meantime, someone else (for example, Nymphidius Sabinus, the prefect of the Praetorian Guard who first compelled his men to change sides and serve Galba) could help himself to the power.

But Galba was not happy to support anyone's ambitions and proved ungrateful to those who enabled him to get to the throne. First, he eliminated those who did not accept him immediately and devastated their cities. Then he executed numerous senators and replaced the troop commanders. He also refused to pay the soldiers what had been promised to them. With the exception of a few inexperienced men who got promoted, everyone was angry. One of the men who supported Galba at first but was insulted by his actions later was Otho. Otho once hoped that Galba would adopt him and make him his heir, but that never happened, so he took matters into his own hands.

Otho

Otho used to be Nero's close friend, until the late emperor seduced, married, and eventually beat to death his former wife, Poppaea. He knew how things functioned at the top, and since he learned that he would never become an heir, he came up with another plan. Otho bought the support of the Praetorian Guard for a large amount of money. Galba, with no supporters whatsoever, was murdered almost instantly.

On 15 January AD 69, Otho had himself declared an emperor. The Senate gladly gave the consent. Even though he was overly ambitious and selfish, Otho had never shown a single sign of ruthless brutality that characterized his precedents. Just as expected, Otho tried to restore stability, peace, and progress. But his reign was not a long one; it lasted a mere three months, ending with a major military defeat and suicide.

Vitellius

The legions of Germania Inferior rejected to promise loyalty to Galba who never paid any rewards to them. On January 1 AD 69, two weeks before Otho got the support of the Senate, they hailed Vitelius, the governor of Germania Inferior, as their emperor.

Vitellius wasn't a spectacularly skilled military leader, but he had the finest Roman legions, including the veterans of the Germanic Wars, on his side. He attacked Otho and crushed him in the Battle of Bedriacum. The damage on Otho's troops and his reputation as a military leader was so severe that he decided it would be better to kill himself than to try and fight Vitellius again. After doing so, Vitellius became the emperor, but not a great one. Suetonius reports that he used to enjoy three banquets a day and spent money on triumphal parades.[73] However, the empire was close to bankruptcy and he needed more funds. Since there were several people who named Vitellius as their heir, he came to the idea to kill them all—and any eventual co-heir—and grab the inheritance. As for those who asked for the money he owed them, he tortured and executed them.

This cruel and incompetent emperor quickly lost the support of men who brought him to the title. He fired nearly the entire Praetorian Guard and was ruining everything, yet he had no idea that his days were numbered.

Vespasian

Vitellius was not the only Roman province governor whose legions decided to support him over the legitimate emperor in Rome. Vespasian had many legions under his command, thanks to Nero when he him a special command in Judaea to deal with the Great Jewish Revolt in AD 67. Both Vespasian and his son Titus were capable soldiers, and the armies they led were loyal to them. In addition to these forces, the future emperor had the support of Gaius Licinus Mucianus, the governor of Syria. Together, they waited for the right moment to return to Rome, with other provinces joining them as well. In October AD 69, the Second Battle of Bedriacum took place. The Danubian legions under the command of Marcus Antonius Primus, who also acclaimed Vespasian as emperor, invaded Italy and devastated Vitellius' army. On December 21 AD 69, the Senate acknowledged the obvious fact. Vespasian was now the true emperor of Rome.

Chapter 5 – The Flavians

The Flavian dynasty was quite an unusual one. For one, it consisted of one man and his sons. The sons of Titus Flavius Vespasianus, Titus and Domitian, had no heirs to succeed them so the dynasty that started with their father ended with them. Another unusual fact is that Vespasian did not come from an aristocratic family, but rather an equestrian one. That was unthinkable in the previous centuries but had become possible in the Year of the Four Emperors.

Caesar and Augustus were no longer family names after Galba; they had become titles. The emperors of Rome held the title "Augustus," and their named heirs were "Caesars." When Vespasian became the emperor, Titus and Domitian were named Caesars.

The First Flavian: Vespasian

Vespasian's parents were equestrians—his father was a banker and tax collector—but Vespasian and his brother Sabinus managed to earn a promotion to senatorial status. Vespasian held a number of public offices and was a consul in AD 51. The detail that distinguished him from other public officials was his extraordinary military success. He was in command of a legion that made the Roman invasion of Britain in AD 43 a triumph, and also dealt with the Jewish rebellion and subjugation of Judaea in AD 66.

Vespasian remained in Judaea until the second half of AD 69, when he gained the huge support of the governors of other provinces who shared a common goal - getting rid of Vitellius. In alliance with them, he stopped the year of civil war in Rome by defeating Vitellius. Once he became the emperor, he worked hard on restoring prosperity. He wasn't obsessed with power and magnificence. Vespasian reorganized institutions such as censorship. He transformed the Senate, mostly by getting rid of unsuitable senators and letting equestrians into the Senate. Finally, he knew how to preserve the loyalty of the army without paying for it.

The empire was dangerously close to bankruptcy due to the years of incompetent reign, and there were a number of unpopular measures that Vespasian had to take, such as raising taxes and introducing new ones. He also took back the land given to the friends of former emperors and revoked the freedom that Nero granted to Greece. Furthermore, it looks like Vespasian sold offices and allowed many ungrateful things to happen for money. He had many enemies too and survived several conspiracies, but overall, he is remembered in a bright light. His legacy includes many public construction projects, including the Colosseum. Vespasian further encouraged the growth and prosperity of Rome by letting anyone build on sites that fire or ruin had made empty.

Like Augustus, Vespasian was aware of the importance of having influential men of letters on his side. The authors of histories that created our views on the ancient Roman world and gave us plenty of information to ponder on—such as Suetonius and Tacitus—were under Vespasian's protection. They were an important element in Flavian propaganda.

According to an omen, Vespasian was predestined to become the emperor of Rome and the only men who could come after him were his sons. When he died in AD 79, no one wondered who would become the next emperor.

Benevolent yet Unfortunate: Titus

Suetonius and other contemporary historians described Titus as an ideal ruler and exemplary emperor, but we must not forget that they depended on him and his father financially. Titus was rather a man of contradiction. His political and military career, as well as his fairly short reign, were remembered by his triumph over Judaea and the destruction of the Second Temple of Jerusalem (which the Romans celebrated, but Jewish sources described as a monstrous act and provided more evidence of Titus's ruthlessness), some scandals (that stopped once he had become the emperor), and massive natural disasters that hit Rome during his reign.

When Vespasian returned to Rome to become the emperor, the uprising in Judaea was still not over, so Titus remained there and continued to fight the Jews until he finished them and completely destroyed the city of Jerusalem, taking numerous people as slaves. Both the Arch of Titus and Colosseum were built thanks to the wealth from the temple of Jerusalem.

The Flavian Amphitheatre (Colosseum)[74] – the construction began under Vespasian and was finished under Titus.
Ramesh, CC BY-SA 3.0 <https://creativecommons.org/licenses/by-sa/3.0>, via Wikimedia Commons
https://commons.wikimedia.org/wiki/File:Colosseo_-_Through_my_lens_2.jpg

When Titus returned to Rome, Vespasian gave him several titles. The future emperor was his father's co-consul, tribune, and the prefect of the Praetorian Guard. He was quite popular and clearly a perfect heir. At this point, his younger brother Domitian was kept aside.

In *Life of Titus*, Suetonius says that people feared Titus would be another Nero, but he proved them wrong by being an effective emperor. The Romans realized that he was a man of virtue, so they loved and praised him.[75]

The Emperor Titus.[76]
Sailko, CC BY 3.0 <https://creativecommons.org/licenses/by/3.0>, via Wikimedia Commons
https://commons.wikimedia.org/wiki/File:Tito,_70-81_ca,_collez._albani.JPG

Titus indeed did a few fantastic things during his short reign. For centuries, the Roman Empire was plagued by the network of *delatores*, whose job was, in essence, to spy on people and accuse them of treason. Titus ended all trials grounded on treason charges, then he publicly humiliated and expelled all delatores from Rome. Unlike other emperors, Titus did not kill senators that he did not like, nor did he confiscate anyone's land. The first couple months of his reign were a success, but then something terrible happened that no one ever anticipated.

On 24 August AD 79, Mount Vesuvius erupted, destroying several cities around Naples. Pompeii and Herculaneum ended up covered by lava and stone. Thousands of families were instantly dead and buried by the eruption. People from the nearby cities lost homes, land, everything they had. Titus helped the victims through coordinated relief efforts and large donations from the imperial treasury. Then in the spring, while Titus was visiting Pompeii, a fire lasted for three days, destroying large parts of Rome. As if that was not enough, a plague broke out. Again, Titus was wholly committed to helping the victims and to finding the cure for the plague. The memory of Titus's generosity was still very fresh when in September AD 81 he suddenly fell ill and died. No one will ever know whether he was poisoned. The people of Rome mourned him sincerely and his brother, the new emperor, Domitian declared Titus a god.

Patient Opportunist and Competent Emperor: Domitian

Domitian—the last Flavian on the Roman throne—was the youngest son of Vespasian and the brother of Titus, and now it was his turn to become the emperor. During his rule, his autocratic style of governing created hostility between himself and the Senate, whose influence he reduced dramatically.

Domitian.[77]
I, Sailko, CC BY-SA 3.0 <http://creativecommons.org/licenses/by-sa/3.0/>, via Wikimedia Commons
https://commons.wikimedia.org/wiki/File:Domiziano_da_collezione_albani,_fine_del_I_sec._dc._02_cropped.jpg

During the reigns of Vespasian and Titus, Domitian's role was minor and mostly ceremonial. Now that both of them were dead, the Praetorian Guard declared Domitian emperor.

Domitian's reign lasted for 15 years. During that time, Domitian revalued the Roman coinage and boosted up the economy after the long period of deflation. The border defenses of the empire were expanded under his reign, and a massive building and restoration program was initiated in the city of Rome.

Domitian was a remarkably authoritarian emperor who aspired to become the new Augustus. Cultural, religious, and military propaganda reinforced the image of him as an enlightened despot whose mission was to guide the people of Rome into a new era of prosperity and brilliance. The people and army admired him, but the members of the Senate saw him as a tyrant and loathed him. The historians that praised his father and brother so much—Tacitus, Suetonius, and Pliny the Younger—depicted Domitian as a ruthless and paranoid autocrat. But this information should be taken with caution. Those historians belonged to the senatorial elite that were opposed to Domitian, and their views are most likely biased.

Many history scholars, centuries later, concluded that Domitian was slightly cruel, but was also a very efficient ruler who achieved prosperity, peace, and stability, providing a firm ground for another peaceful century.[78] Domitian may have executed and banished some important men, just like everyone else before him (except Titus), but Domitian also rejected aggressive expansionism and negotiated peace whenever he could. He stopped the campaigns against Scotland and Dacia, as those would cause great expenses. His foreign policy was realistic and his goal was stability. Moreover, he did not persecute Jews, Christians, and other religious minorities.

Domitian had the public admiration but was surrounded by enemies. On 18 September AD 96, he was murdered in a plot prepared by court officials. Suetonius wrote about the omens that foretold his death.[79] The man who killed him did not survive, as Domitian fought back and stabbed him, but it didn't really matter. The unpopular ruler was dead and the senators were happy. The soldiers were angry, but that was a small inconvenience for the winners. The Senate decided to punish Domitian by "damnatio memoriae," which means that they ordered the deletion of his name from any inscriptions in the empire. However, as you can see, Domitian was not forgotten.

Chapter 6 – The Nerva-Antonine Dynasty: The Five Good Emperors (and a Couple of Not So Good Ones)

AD 96 started the Nerva-Antonine dynasty which lasted to AD 192. Out of the seven emperors from this dynasty, five are remembered as "The Five Good Emperors," Thanks to Machiavelli.[80] One of the characteristics of this dynasty was that all its emperors— except Nerva and Commodus—were adopted by their predecessors, who chose their heirs by their competence rather than their blood. Hence, these emperors are sometimes referred to as "adoptive emperors." Machiavelli stated in 1503 that "while all the emperors who succeeded to the throne by birth, except Titus, were bad, all were good who succeeded by adoption, as in the case of the five from Nerva to Marcus. But as soon as the empire fell once more to the heirs by birth, its ruin recommenced."[81] Eventually, Marcus Aurelius, the fifth of the five good emperors, named his biological son Commodus as his heir. According to many, this decision caused the decline of the Roman Empire.[82] The Western Empire may have lasted for another three centuries, but the era of glory and prosperity, which flourished during the reign of the Nerva-Antonine dynasty, was gone forever.[83] Until recently, historians praised the wisdom of these emperors who chose men of virtue and not their biological sons as their heirs, implying that there was a sort of "adoptive" ideology behind this. However, there's also the fact that the rulers from this dynasty (except Aurelius) simply had no sons of their own.

The First of the Five: Nerva

After Domitian's death, the Senate and the Praetorian Guard picked Nerva as the next emperor. Nerva was 65 and childless. He was also a distinguished public official from the time of Nero, where he exposed a great conspiracy. He was loyal to the Flavians as well, becoming the consul under both Vespasian and Domitian. Now that the Senate's enemy, Domitian, was dead, it was the first serious opportunity to restore the institutions of the republic and get rid of all emperors once and for all. But they didn't do that, probably because it was easier to just keep the privileges and throw all the responsibility to one man. Nerva seemed perfect for that role.

Nerva was often described as wise and moderate. He really tried to gain support of the people of Rome and spent serious amounts of money trying to do so. Nevertheless, the Roman army wasn't willing to accept him. In October AD 97 the Praetorian Guard revolted against Nerva. They wanted the assassins of Domitian executed, not just fired, but Nerva refused to do so. A contemporary Roman, the consul Fronto, described the time of Nerva's rule as anarchy and stated that even Domitian's tyranny was better.[84]

Nerva proved to be too meek for the role of Roman Emperor. He refused to punish those who conspired against him and ultimately lost any authority over the Senate. Nerva's reign was in deep crisis and he knew it wouldn't last. Prompted to name an heir other than his unqualified relatives, he was planning to adopt the governor of Syria, Marcus Cornelius Nigrinus. But the choice wasn't up to him. The Senate had already chosen the next emperor, a famous military commander, Marcus Ulpius Traianus, or Trajan. Nerva adopted Trajan, and the two men were meant to share consulship in AD 98, but on 1 January that year, Nerva died of a stroke. The Senate instantly made him a god and the reign of one of the most important Roman Emperors began.

The Senate's Favorite—Optimus Princeps (The Best Emperor Ever) Trajan

Both the Senate and the army were enthusiastic about having Trajan as the new emperor, but this choice was a bit controversial. The fact that he wasn't of aristocratic origin didn't matter that much because there had already been a number of emperors from diverse backgrounds. But Trajan wasn't Roman or even entirely Italian, as he came from modern-day Andalusia. According to Cassius Dio,[85] Trajan's mother was Spanish. Other sources say she was not.

Anyhow, he was the chosen one according to an ancient omen.

The story of Trajan begins two years earlier. In late 96 AD, the new emperor Nerva chose Trajan, then just a senator from southern Spain, to control Upper Germania. It was an important assignment, and the custom required Trajan to make a sacrifice to Rome's chief deity, Jupiter. The entrance to Jupiter's shrine was crowded, and it wasn't easy for Trajan to get through. Finally, he opened the temple doors, revealing Jupiter's statue within. At that very moment, the crowd unexpectedly shouted, "Imperator!"[86]

The Roman Emperor Trajan.[87]
Thomas Ihle, CC BY-SA 3.0 <http://creativecommons.org/licenses/by-sa/3.0/>, via Wikimedia Commons https://commons.wikimedia.org/wiki/File:Trajan-Xanten.JPG

In October AD 97, Trajan was given a note from Nerva, letting him know of his adoption. Trajan knew very well what was going on in Rome and wanted to take care of the delicate situation. He sent for the conspirators within the Praetorian Guard, those who wanted

Domitian's killers dead and had engineered the mutiny against Nerva, and gave them a special commission. His intent, according to Cassius Dio,[88] was to keep them busy and put them out of his way.

When Nerva died, Trajan did not hurry to Rome. First, he checked the Rhine and Danube frontiers to make sure they were safe from the Dacians. Besides, he needed to test the dependability of several legions that were still loyal to Domitian. When everything was set up, in the summer of AD 99, he entered Rome on foot and joined the senators and other people of Rome who expected him so eagerly.

Although he kept an excellent relationship with the Senate, Trajan was seen as an benevolent autocrat, unlike unpopular Domitian. His fairness, bravery, and the simplicity of his habits were striking.[89] He cared about good government and the public prosperity, established a generous domestic policy, and rehabilitated the prisoners and exiles from previous decades. Trajan provided the *alimenta* (financial aid and free corn) for poor families, reduced taxes, and initiated a large project of public buildings. The dilapidated road system was restored, and new bridges, baths, aqueducts, and other public buildings were constructed.

Trajan was a thoughtful emperor but wasn't quite a pacifist. This man loved war and was a remarkably good soldier. He defeated the Dacians, who had caused much hassle to Domitian and others, twice, in AD 101 and again in 105,because the Dacian king Decebalus did not respect the peace agreement. Over half a million Dacians had to leave their land and make room for a similar number of Romans. The Land of the Romans (Romania) was created where the kingdom of Dacia used to be. This was a major victory and Trajan celebrated with a series of gladiatorial contests. Over 10,000 gladiators fought to death, and even more animals were killed.

The next six years were relatively peaceful. However, in AD 114, the new enemy from the East, the Parthians took over Armenia on the eastern frontier of the Empire. Trajan's army took it back, then proceeded to the east and took Mesopotamia. During the reign of Trajan, the Roman Empire was bigger than ever and stretched from Scotland to the Caspian Sea.

In AD 117, several rebellions broke out in both the east and the north. On the way from one front to another, Trajan fell ill, perhaps due to poison, and died in Cilicia. His body was transferred to Rome, cremated, and buried at the base of the great Trajan's Column.

Trajan was married to Pompeia Plotina, but the couple had no children whatsoever. Cassius Dio and modern historians believe that Trajan was homosexual.[90] One of his putative lovers was his adopted son Hadrian, whom Trajan made his successor under very strange circumstances on his deathbed.

The Provinces' Favorite—Hadrian

Hadrian's relationship with Trajan was not perfect. He had become a part of the family by marrying Trajan's grandniece, but Trajan himself had never shown any intention of making him his heir. Then, dying on his bed, Trajan reportedly adopted him by means of a simple deathbed wish, stated before no other witnesses but his wife Plotina and Prefect Attianus, who was speculated to be Plotina's lover. Plotina signed the adoption document. Stories and speculations circulated from that day onwards, but no one will ever know what really happened.

The Roman Emperor Hadrian.[91]
Livioandronico2013, CC BY-SA 4.0 <https://creativecommons.org/licenses/by-sa/4.0>, via Wikimedia Commons https://commons.wikimedia.org/wiki/File:Busts_of_Hadrianus_in_Venice_cropped.jpg

Regardless, as the Senate did not want another civil war, the legitimacy of the adoption was not disputed. The military was the first to acclaim Hadrian emperor, and the Senate soon followed. In return, Hadrian gave the customary bonus to the legions, to reward their loyalty. But the senators weren't happy when he executed four of them without any trial, simply based on the word of the Prefect Attianus who said they had been preparing a conspiracy. By the end of his reign, Hadrian's relations with the Senate were delicate, even though he promised he'd never execute someone based on unfounded accusations again and made someone else the prefect shortly afterward.

Hadrian spent more time in the provinces than in Rome. Since Trajan had stretched the borders of the empire further than ever before, numerous revolts were breaking out one after another. In fact, in the moment of Trajan's death and his ascension, Hadrian was dealing with the rebellion on the Danube frontier.

Once he had become the emperor, Hadrian stopped further expansion of the empire. Just like his distant predecessor Augustus, he believed that the empire should stay firm within its borderlines. Further expansion by those who ruled in the interim, from Claudius to Trajan, had only created problems and the empire had to put huge effort into maintaining its borders. Hadrian went on a tour of the provinces to make sure everything was in order. Military discipline was of the highest importance, and he reorganized the frontiers. In Britain, he built the famous Wall "to separate Romans from barbarians."[92] He even returned the provinces that he believed were too much to handle, like Armenia and Mesopotamia.

As for the provinces that remained within the empire, Hadrian gave them considerable autonomy and fostered their growth and the development of their cities. He designed or personally sponsored countless civil and religious buildings. In Rome, he completed the Pantheon and built the large Temple of Venus and Roma. But his work on restoration extended to Egypt, Greece, and other provinces. Hadrian was a philhellene and his wish was to make Athens the cultural capital of the empire. Many magnificent temples were built and even more of them were restored throughout Greece.

Hadrian's reign was mostly peaceful, but there was one great exception. While the Greeks were thrilled by Hadrian's restoration works, the Jews in Judaea were not. They were considerably upset by the attempts to assimilate them into the Graeco-Roman world and revolted. The Bar Kokhba revolt in Judaea was ferocious with many dead on both sides, and it ended catastrophically for the Jews. Hadrian took away their land and removed the name Judaea, naming the province Syria Palaestina. Jerusalem was rebuilt in Greek style and named Aelia Capitolina.

Hadrian's personal life was marked by the unhappy marriage with Sabina and the warm friendship and possible love affair with the Greek Antinous who died young, which made the emperor weep like a woman.[93] Hadrian died of heart failure in AD 138 and was succeeded by his adopted son Antoninus.

The Respectful Emperor—Antoninus Pius

Antoninus Pius ("dutiful") was a just and kindhearted man. He was admired by everyone in the empire, including both the common people and the elite. His reign lasted for 23 years, and for most of the time, it was a peaceful one.

Hadrian adopted Antoninus, but only after Lucius Ceionius Commodus, who was Hadrian's initial choice, died of tuberculosis. Antoninus wasn't even his second choice; it was Marcus Aurelius. But Marcus was only 16 at the time, and Antoninus, an elderly and highly esteemed public official, seemed like a safe choice. In February AD 138, Hadrian adopted him and made him his heir, but the condition was that Antoninus must adopt his favorites, Marcus Aurelius and Lucius Verus, in turn.

Antoninus' reign was a surprise for everyone. It not only lasted much longer than anyone anticipated, but was also highly efficient. Cassius Dio described him as a "noble and good" man who never oppressed anyone.[94] Antoninus was grateful to Hadrian, had him deified, and intended to simply continue with his policies. But unlike Hadrian, he ruled from the safety of Rome, allowing his loyal commanders to handle the minor conflicts in Egypt, Germania, and Mauritania.

Antoninus insisted on a fair and impartial administration of justice. He went so far as to free many of the men Hadrian had imprisoned (he was certain that this had been Hadrian's wish). Antoninus was also a frugal ruler who held the finances under strict control, and at the time of his death, there was a huge surplus in the budget. Trade and commerce increased. Many Hadrian's construction projects were finished and quite a few new added, including the temples he built in memory of his loving wife, Faustina, and of Hadrian. A new wall (the Antonine Wall) was built in Scotland.

The Last of the Good Ones—Marcus Aurelius

"People exist for the sake of one another; teach them, then, or bear with them."

—Marcus Aurelius[95]

Antoninus died in AD 161. His wife and most of his children, including two sons, were already dead. The title of emperor now belonged to Marcus Aurelius and Lucius Verus.

Marcus Aurelius was the emperor of Rome from AD 161 to 180. Lucius Verus ruled jointly with Aurelius until his death in AD 169, and in 177 Aurelius made his son Commodus a co-emperor.

Aurelius is best known as the Stoic philosopher and the author of *Meditations*. As an emperor, he epitomized the Platonic ideal, which is a wise ruler utilizing his power to help people rather than to help himself.

The Roman Emperor Marcus Aurelius.[96]
https://commons.wikimedia.org/wiki/File:Marcus_Aurelius_Metropolitan_Museum.png

This wise man was not just a philosopher. He had an active role as supreme commander. During the latter part of his reign, he spent most of his time on the battlefields in central Europe protecting the Danube frontier against various barbarian tribes. There he wrote many notes that later became a part of *Meditations*, an intimate diary influenced by the philosophy of the Greek thinker, Epictetus.

At the same time, his co-ruler Lucius Verus fought the Parthians, defending Syria and Armenia. The Romans won, but this war was followed by plague and, afterward, famine. The following years were full of trouble on the borders, which made the situation even harder. In AD

169, Lucius Verus died. Marcus Aurelius continued to fight bravely until AD 180. With the war against the Parthians almost won, he died at Vindobona (present-day Vienna, Austria). His son Commodus fought with him, not just as his heir, but as his equal. He had already been declared Marcus's co-emperor in AD 177.

The End or Not Quite Yet? Commodus

AD 180 was not the year when the Roman Empire ceased to exist and Commodus was not its last ruler, but historians of all periods agree that the ascension of Commodus marks the end of Rome as we know it, a highly organized society and an invincible superforce. The historian Cassius Dio, who witnessed the change, said "our history now descends from a kingdom of gold to one of iron and rust."[97] One of the most respected researchers of ancient Rome today, Mary Beard, finishes her superb book, *SPQR: A History of Ancient Rome* with Commodus,[98] as if there was nothing else left worth mentioning. The magnificent empire with a republican past gradually transformed into something else, and a few centuries later, finally collapsed. And the fall happened to start with this emperor.

Commodus wasn't the worst emperor ever. One can hardly be worse than Caligula or Nero. But back then, thanks to the previous efforts of Augustus and Tiberius, Rome could sustain Caligula and Nero. Similarly, many agree that Domitian made the prosperity in the time of the five good emperors possible. Now, the situation was different—the enemies at all frontiers grew stronger year after year and Rome was struggling. One incompetent emperor would mean a catastrophe. And Commodus fit that description.

First of all, Commodus was extremely underage for any of the roles that were given to him. In AD 176, he became an imperator and a tribune. In 177, he was an emperor and consul. There once was a formal request that one should be at least 32 years old to become a consul; Commodus was 15. By the time of his 32nd birthday, he managed to get murdered (to everyone's relief).

At the beginning, it didn't look like he was going to be a disastrous ruler. Commodus had been raised with high hopes and the finest education, but ended up being an egomaniac that took part in gladiatorial games and loved to be depicted as Hercules (as a matter of fact, he believed he was the incarnation of the deity). He wasn't interested in boring jobs and administration, so he let a few men run everything. One of those men was a freedman called Cleander, who came to the idea to sell consulships and actually did exactly that - he sold consulships for 25 years in advance. Meanwhile, people were killed for obscure reasons, from treason charges to the fact that they were just better athletes than the emperor. He also had the bright idea to rename the empire to Commodiana. The value of Roman coins was devalued, plague broke out, and it looked like all the misfortunes of the world were strangling Rome.

Commodus as Hercules.[99]
https://commons.wikimedia.org/wiki/File:Commodus_Musei_Capitolini_MC1120.jpg

Finally, when in AD 192 the prefect of the Praetorian Guard, Aemilius Laetus, and the Chamberlain, Eclectus, heard that Commodus was planning to have both consuls executed in order to replace them with gladiators, they decided to kill him. It was 31 December AD 192 and everyone was distracted by the Saturnalia, the important yearly festival. Commodus' mistress gave him poisoned wine, but the emperor was already so drunk that he vomited the poison up. Since that plan didn't work, Commodus' personal trainer strangled him.

Chapter 7 – Some New Emperors

Commodus, unsurprisingly, left no successor. Another important dynasty had ended and opened space for all kinds of opportunists. Those who had organized Commodus' murder went to the consul, Publius Helvius Pertinax. Pertinax was the son of a freedman, became an equestrian, and then a senator during the reign of Marcus Aurelius. He was wealthy and experienced in governing provinces such as Africa and Britain. He made a deal with the Praetorians, offering them large bonuses and promising he would reintroduce discipline, so they made him emperor.

Ambitious, Capable, and Not Quite Legitimate: Pertinax

Pertinax reorganized government and declared himself "Chief of the Senate." Then he declared the deceased Commodus a public enemy, knocking down all his statues and selling his possessions so that he could raise money for the soldiers. But soldiers weren't happy about the idea of having someone restore order and bring discipline to the ranks. Under Commodus, they were allowed to get drunk and behave however they wanted, which included hitting people on the street. Meanwhile, the Praetorians who made Pertinax emperor came to the idea to replace him with another consul. When the conspiracy against Pertinax failed, they went to the soldiers and told them they were going to be put to death by the emperor. They panicked and promptly killed the emperor.

How Much for an Empire? Didius Julianus

Another former consul who had enough cash to bribe the Praetorians and become an emperor was Didius Julianus. He won the empire at an open auction, where the city prefect Sulpicianus almost outbid him. Didius enjoyed his days as emperor by spending public money on banquets and handing out favors, until a crowd demanded that someone save them from Didius, who spent the funds that were supposed to be used —namely the legions under the governor Pescennius Niger in Syria. The men of the aforementioned Pescennius declared him emperor. Other troops did the same, declaring their governors, Clodius Albinus and Lucius Septimius Severus, as emperors. A civil war was about to begin, but Severus came up with a cunning plan. He faked a friendship with Clodius Albinus, promising to make him his declared heir. Albinus swallowed it and stayed in Britain while Severus marched on Rome.

As for Didius, he is remembered by the shortest reign in the history of the Roman Empire, 66 days, and his cries as he was executed: "What evil have I done? Whom have I killed?"[100]

The Founder of a New Dynasty: Septimius Severus

Septimus Severus was a senator under Marcus Aurelius. Later, when under Commodus, Cleander sold consulships and Severus bought one. He believed he was predestined to be an emperor, dreaming about it and seeing signs of omens everywhere. Now that he got rid of Didius, he went to the east and defeated Niger and anyone who seemed like a supporter of anyone but himself. Albinus realized he had been deceived, and the two armies fought in AD 197 with Severus winning. Severus ordered Albinus's wife, children, and all his supporters to be killed. Shortly thereafter, he purged the Senate and prepared to establish a dynasty, but at the same time he claimed to be the son of Marcus Aurelius. He then renamed his son Bassianus to Marcus Aurelius Antoninus, but he remained known by his nickname Caracalla, which was a kind of Gallic hooded tunic that he usually wore and made fashionable.

Severus died in AD 211, succeeded by his sons Caracalla and Geta whom he had already made co-emperors.

Another Spoiled Kid: Caracalla

Caracalla was said to be smart and compassionate as a child, but later he turned into an arrogant and ambitious oppressor who hated his brother and loved to think of himself as Alexander the Great.

Caracalla had actually already tried to kill his father; now that Severus was dead, this princeps had all his advisors killed. Then he killed his wife, brother (in their mother's room), and anyone else who looked like a threat in his imagination. No one but himself was allowed to have any power. In AD 212, he gave Roman citizenship to all men within the borders of the empire, only to make them pay the increased taxes. Most of the money he spent on the army. Caracalla was extremely bloodthirsty and enjoyed seeing people killed. Eventually, he got killed by the next emperor, who proved himself to be even worse than Caracalla.

Caucious, but Not Enough: Macrinus

Marcus Opelius Macrinus was a man of modest background from Mauretania in North Africa. He worked hard to achieve equestrian status and became a reputable lawyer. He was in fact so good that he was given charge of Caracalla's property. Eventually, he became prefect of the Praetorian Guard and was equally successful in the new position.

An African oracle said that Macrinus and his son were preordained to be emperors. Macrinus wasn't superstitious, but Caracalla was and would have him assassinated if he heard about the prophecy. So, he quickly arranged a plot and had Caracalla killed on a campaign. But he wanted his hands clean and made sure it looked like soldiers killed Caracalla and that he had nothing to do with it.

Macrinus deified Caracalla, took the name Severus, added Antoninus to his son Diadumenian's name, and acted as if they were part of the Severan (and indirectly the Antonine) dynasty.

But Macrinus was merely an equestrian and he had never gotten to the senatorial rank. This was not the only thing that made him unpopular. He also made an unforgivable mistake: he lost Roman territory; unable to keep Armenia within the borders, he had to give it up and hand it over to the Parthians. Moreover, he promoted a former spy, Adventus, to consul and prefect of Rome, even though the man had no basic understanding of how the Roman institutions worked. Macrinus' behavior, such as flaunting his gold and jewels, alienated the soldiers as well.

Lastly, he did not get rid of the Severans thoroughly enough. Julia Domna, Septimus Severus' widow and mother to Caracalla, had a sister whose grandsons, Elagabalus and Severus Alexander, seemed like great candidates for the throne. Macrinus sent troops to kill Elagabalus, but the soldiers decided to change sides. The emperor and his son were promptly executed.

The Son-God Aficionado: Elagabalus

Elagabalus' name was changed to Marcus Aurelius Antoninus, although he had no connection with the Antonine dynasty. He was 14 years old in AD 218 when he became emperor, thanks to the cash that his grandmother gave to the soldiers. Elagabalus' mother and grandmother were effectively in charge.

Elagabalus worshiped the Syrian sun-god Heliogabalus, brought the sacral stone to Rome, and built a temple to the sun-god. He wasn't interested in Roman administration and institutions, but he sold offices to affluent men, no matter how incompetent they were.

One day, Elagabalus came to the idea to have his cousin and adopted heir, Alexanius, killed. The soldiers disobeyed and rescued the said Alexanius (later known as Severus Alexander) and his family. Elagabalus tried it again in AD 222, and the Praetorians killed him and his mother instead, dragging their bodies all over Rome and then throwing them in the Tiber. No Roman ruler, however corrupt, had been ever degraded that way before.

Mom's Little Boy: Severus Alexander

Alexanius—Marcus Aurelius Severus Alexander from now on—was only 13 when he was declared emperor. Until his grandmother's death in AD 226, he was under her influence. After that, he obeyed his mother, Julia Mamaea. Julia was an intelligent woman and was well aware that her and Alexander's lives would be in danger if another period of military anarchy came. She knew that good relations with the Senate would make her rule more stable, so she established the imperial council. 16 senators were appointed to this council, and one of them, the great lawyer Domitius Ulpianus, was made the Praetorian prefect. In reality, this man, under Mamaea's supervision, was in charge of the government of the Roman Empire. The empire briefly returned to stability and sanity. For a period of ten years, the borderlines were undisturbed, aid was given to the urban mob (people from different parts of the empire who - or whose ancestors centuries ago - had become poor due to debt and came to Rome), *alimentia* (the aid in corn and other goods) was increased, and special funds for teachers were made—and the Roman economy sustained all these expenses.

But Rome was to face a major external challenge. The Sassanids (a Persian dynasty) were coming, determined to retake the territory that was once the land of the Persians. And much of the Roman Empire on the east used to be Persian. Alexander won a battle against them, but with serious consequences. At the same time, Germanic tribes took the opportunity to revolt. Alexander was on the way to the German border when his own troops mutinied in AD 234. They supported Maximinus Thrax ("Maximinus the Thracian"), a skillful military commander, and soon after that Alexander and his mother were killed.

Chapter 8 – Crises, Civil Wars, and Divisions: The Long and Painful Decline

In the third century, the Roman Empire became fragmented. During the so-called Crisis of the Third Century or the Imperial Crisis (AD 235-284), three breakaway political entities emerged: the Gallic Empire, the Roman Empire, and the Palmyrene Empire. Social turmoil and chaos characterized the period. Over 20 emperors rose and fell in just 50 years until Emperor Aurelian and, the later Diocletian managed to end the crisis and find a model for the survival of the empire.

When Septimus Severus began to buy the loyalty of the soldiers through increased pay, he also degraded the value of the coinage; since his descendants did the same, the economy of the state weakened. At the same time, he made the role of the emperor too dependent on the loyalty of the army. This became a serious issue when Alexander Severus, under the influence of his mother, chose to pay the Germanic tribes for peace instead of suppressing them. The army had already lost respect for him, and this cowardly act came as the final insult. The soldiers killed both mother and son, and Maximinus Thrax took charge.

The Thracian soldier Maximinus Thrax (235-238 CE) became the first of the so-called "Barracks Emperors" who would come and go quickly throughout the crisis of the next 49 years.

The Barracks Emperors

Rather than a dynasty, the "Barracks Emperors" refers to the group of third-century Roman emperors who came from the army and were chosen based on their popularity and generosity towards their troops. Those emperors were also expected to give immediate and evident results. There were no heirs or chance for succession: any incompetent emperor was killed and replaced by another.

There were over 20 emperors between the reign of Alexander Severus and that of Diocletian. Maximinus Thrax (AD 235-238) was eventually killed by his troops when they were exhausted from the persistent warfare he continued pushing them into. Also, they had noticed that he was an ineffective leader when confronted with plague, famine, and massive civil conflict.

Gordian I and Gordian II (co-emperors of Rome during the spring of AD 238) were a father and son who tried to overthrow Maximinus with the consent of the Senate. Gordian II was killed in a fight against pro-Maximinus forces, and his father killed himself upon hearing of his death.

Balbinus and Pupienus (co-emperors of Rome in early summer of AD 238) also fought Maximinus, but were fairly unpopular and ended up being killed by the Praetorian Guard.

Gordian III (AD 238-244) co-ruled with Balbinus and Pupienus. When they were killed, he was proclaimed emperor by the military supporters of Gordian I and Gordian II. He was liquidated, most likely by Philip the Arab.

Philip the Arab (AD 244-249) was the Praetorian prefect turned emperor. He declared his son, Philip II, his co-emperor. He was murdered in battle by Decius, and the Praetorian Guard killed his 12-year old son shortly after that.

Decius (AD 249-251) was a regional governor until his troops made him an emperor. He also hoped his son, Herennius Etruscus, would succeed him, but both died at the Battle of Abritus in 251. Decius's younger son, Hostilian (AD 251, June-November), died in office from the plague.

Gallus (AD 251-253) and his son and co-emperor, Volusianus, were murdered by their own troops.

Aemilianus (fall of AD 253) was a regional governor chosen to replace Gallus but proved incompetent and was killed in favor of Valerian.

Valerian (AD 253-260) died as the prisoner of the Sassanid Persians. He was the first Roman Emperor to be seized as a prisoner of war. His capturing during the negotiations of truce caused shock and instability throughout the Empire.

Gallienus (AD 253-268), the son and co-emperor of Valerian, was a successful emperor and military leader who introduced many developments in the military and culture. In spite of that, he was killed by his own troops on a campaign in a scheme involving the future emperor Aurelian.

Claudius Gothicus (AD 268-270), famous at the time for his victories over the Goths, wasn't thrilled to accept the position of emperor and was said to have avenged the death of Gallienus. He was rather effective, but only two years into his reign he died of the plague. His brother Quintillus (AD 270) succeeded him but was killed shortly after.

Aurelian (AD 270-275) is remembered as one of the few Barracks Emperors determined to place the public well-being and protection of the empire above his personal ambition. He reunited the empire by crushing the Gallic and Palmyrene breakaway empires and taking them back under Roman control. He also dealt successfully with several hostile tribes. Even so, he was assassinated by his commanders.

The Breakaway Empires

In AD 260 Postumus, the regional governor of Upper and Lower Germania was made emperor of the so-called Gallic Empire (Germania, Gaul, Hispania, and Britannia). A decade later, Queen Zenobia of Palmyra formed her own empire in the east, the Palmyrene (Syria and Egypt). They never rebelled against Rome. Instead, they assured the Senate of Rome that this was in Rome's best interest. Instead of fighting with each other to attain the title of Roman emperor, they had chosen to rule their provinces the best they could. The barrack emperors paid no attention to these provinces as they were too busy fighting each other. But Aurelian did pay attention and wasn't interested in listening about the political motives behind these empires. He marched into Egypt, seized Zenobia, and took the territory without ruining the city. Then he went to the west to battle Postumus, who was already dead at the time, but his successor, Tetricus I, was overwhelmed by Aurelian. Eventually, Aurelian managed to restore the empire, albeit shortly. His commanders believed that he planned to eliminate and replace them, so they killed him. A few more emperors emerged and fell, and with them, the Principate ended, although this type of rule had already been profoundly degenerated. It was time for serious change.

The same paradigm existed during the next nine years until Diocletian took power. While they were fighting each other over who was supposed to rule, employing increasingly expanding armies and more supplies, the empire they wanted to lead was breaking apart. The Roman economy could not support such expenses, and the currency was deflating, creating social chaos.

Chapter 9 – Two Empires: East and West

In AD 285, Emperor Diocletian divided the Roman Empire in half, creating the Western Roman Empire and the Eastern Roman Empire (or the Byzantine Empire). He believed that the major cause of the Imperial Crisis was a lack of clarity in succession, so he ordered that successors must be selected and approved from the beginning of an individual's rule. Diocletian decided to retire from rule in AD 305, and some of his successors, especially the generals Maxentius and Constantine who weren't his immediate heirs, pushed the empire again into civil war.

Diocletian and the Tetrarchy

Diocletian was born as Diocles in a poor family in Dalmatia. Thanks to his high capabilities and merit, he rose through the ranks of the military. He came to power in AD 284 and the next year made Maximian his co-emperor. Diocletian believed that such a large and unstable empire required more than one emperor and that the territories should be split. He continued to rule the Greek East, and Maximian was in charge of the Latin West. Then in 293 he went even further and created the Tetrarchy (the rule of four men). He picked two among the most promising men in the army and made them Caesars (junior emperors). Constantinus would help Maximian in the west and Galerius would help Diocletian. The plan was that after a certain timeframe the two senior emperors would abdicate with the juniors succeeding them and naming their own juniors immediately.

The four tetrarchs had new headquarters; none were based in Rome, however, since it was too far from the areas these men were keeping safe from aggressive barbarians. Diocletian was emperor for 20 years when he visited Rome for the first time in AD 303. His head office was in Nicomedia in Asia Minor (present-day Turkey), Maximian ruled from Milan in Italy, Constantius was based in Trier in Gaul, and Galerius in Sirmium (present-day Serbia).

Diocletian and Maximian restored cities and infrastructure energetically, reformed the army and provinces, introduced a completely different kind of tax (in goods rather than in cash) and finally introduced the Dominate, a new totalitarian political system that became the base for later feudalism.

In 303 Diocletian and Maximian started persecuting Christians systematically, devastating churches and confiscating holy texts, but the people were mostly spared—maybe because Diocletian's wife was Christian.

The End of the Tetrarchy

Diocletian and Maximian retired in AD 305. Constantinus and Galerius succeeded them and named their junior Caesars. The naming of their successors left many disappointed and angry though. Galerius had chosen Maximinus II Daia and not his son Maxentius. Constantine also picked someone else—Severus II—rather than his son Constantine. Diocletian's adopted son, Licinius, was left out too.

But when Constantinus died in AD 306, his troops ignored Severus II and declared Constantine emperor—an act crucial for the history of the world. Galerius was angry but determined to avoid civil war. He came to the idea to make Severus II emperor in the west with Constantine becoming his junior and heir. Maxentius intervened too and his father returned from retirement. Severus II went to fight the usurpers, but his men changed sides, and he ended up being killed. Maximian tried to make his son calm down by marrying his daughter to Constantine. During the short period of chaos, Maxentius—who declared himself an emperor three times—was declared a public enemy.

The Christian Emperor—Constantine

In AD 312, at the Battle of the Milvian Bridge, Constantine crushed Maxentius and became the only emperor of both the Western and Eastern Empires. He firmly believed that Jesus Christ had helped him win and introduced a series of decrees and laws, such as the Edict of Milan (AD 317), ordering religious tolerance, especially for Christianity.

Earlier Roman emperors used to claim a relationship with a god to enhance their authority. Instead of Jupiter or some Egyptian deity (which were very fashionable once), Constantine selected Jesus Christ. He presided over the First Council of Nicea (AD 325), which gathered to organize the faith and resolve major issues, such as the divinity of Jesus and authenticity of holy texts. The members of the council selected the manuscripts which were to be collected, in order to create The Bible. The empire was stabilized, the currency revalued, and the army reformed again. On top of all, Constantine founded New Rome—a new city on the location of the former city of Byzantium (present-day Istanbul) which was soon renamed to Constantinople.

Constantine has ever since been celebrated as Constantine the Great, but he could not save the fallen empire from chaos. Soon after his death, his three sons split the Roman Empire between them and fought over which of them deserved more. Only Constantius II survived and was followed by Julian, a Neo-Platonic philosopher who rejected Christianity and held Constantine responsible for the decline of the empire. He banned the Christian teachings and spread of the religion. But after his death, Christianity was reestablished as the dominant faith of the empire under Jovian and especially under Theodosius I (AD 379-395), who continued Constantine's and Jovian's reforms, closed "pagan" schools and universities (such as Plato's Academy), and turned temples into churches. Theodosius I was so dedicated to promoting Christianity that his other duties as emperor seem to have been neglected. As a result, he was the last to rule both the Eastern and Western Empires.

The Fall of The Roman Empire

During the period from AD 376 to 382, Rome fought numerous battles against aggressive Goths (the Gothic Wars). On 9 August AD 378, at the Battle of Adrianople, the Roman Emperor Valens was overwhelmed. This event was critical in the weakening of the Western Roman Empire. Many debated that Christianity was a major cause in the empire's fall. Others said it was paganism. Most likely, the problems were rooted in the corruption of the governing class and the impossibility to rule such a vast empire effectively. The arrival of the Visigoths in the third century AD and their successive uprisings proved detrimental.

On 4 September AD 476, the Germanic King Odoacer overthrew the Roman Emperor Romulus Augustus, and the Western Roman Empire officially ceased to exist. The Eastern Roman Empire (the Byzantine Empire) continued its life until AD 1453. At first, it was known as simply "the Roman Empire," but it was a completely different entity. The Western Roman Empire was reinvented centuries later as The Holy Roman Empire, but again had nothing to do with the Roman Empire of antiquity. That story had ended forever.

Conclusion

After the fall of the Western Roman Empire, Europe broke into a number of little kingdoms and regions. The rivalry between the kings created a state of constant war. The threat of invasion was ongoing, and the borders were continuously changed. In the Middle Ages, even cities fought one another. At the same time, in the east, another empire of the same name - The Roman Empire - flourished until the rise of the Ottomans in the 15th century.

Nowadays, dozens of independent countries exist in the territory of what was once the Roman Empire. The influence of the Roman Empire profoundly affected all aspects of modern western culture. Its vast legacy, including the political system that Rome created, persists throughout the world. Our cultural values, as well as our deepest religious beliefs, have their origin in ancient Rome. Many words that we use, regardless of our native language, come from Latin. Finally, our notions of civilization—with all its inevitable decadent elements—are shaped in Rome. The history of Rome is not just the history of a city in the Mediterranean region. It is rather the first chapter in the history of today's global world.

Timeline of Important Events

44 BC (15 March) – Assassination of Julius Caesar: Caesar was killed in the Theatre of Pompey by the "Liberators."

43 BC (27 November   ) – The Second Triumvirate: Octavian, Mark Antony and Marcus Aemilius Lepidus (triumvir) were granted the power to make and annul laws and appoint magistrates.

42 BC - Liberators' civil war: Octavian and Antony led armies to northern Greece pursuing Caesar's assassins Brutus and Cassius. Brutus was killed.

33 BC – The end of the Second Triumvirate

31 BC – Battle of Actium: Octavian defeated Antony and Cleopatra in a naval battle.

30 BC – Antony's forces defected to Octavian. Antony and Cleopatra committed suicide.

27 BC – Octavian becomes Augustus

21 BC – Augustus married his only daughter Julia to Marcus Vipsanius Agrippa.

17 BC – Augustus adopted the sons of Agrippa and Julia

12 BC – Germanic Wars; Agrippa died.

11 BC – Augustus married Julia to Tiberius.

6 BC – Augustus offered Tiberius tribunician power and imperium over the eastern half of the Empire. Tiberius refused, announcing his retirement to Rhodes.

2 BC – The Senate acclaimed Augustus Pater Patriae (father of the country)

AD 2 – Tiberius returned to Rome as a private citizen.

AD 4 – Augustus adopted Tiberius.

AD 13 – Tiberius became co-princeps.

AD 14 – Augustus died. Germanicus was appointed commander of Roman forces in Germania.

AD 16 – Germanicus defeated a Germanic force on the Weser.

AD 18 – Tiberius granted Germanicus imperium over the eastern half of the Empire.

AD 19 – Germanicus died in Antioch, most likely poisoned on Tiberius's orders.

AD 22 – Tiberius granted Drusus Julius Caesar tribunician power, marking him as his choice as successor.

AD 37 – Tiberius died, leaving his offices jointly to Caligula and Tiberius Gemellus.

AD 38 – Tiberius Gemellus was assassinated on Caligula's orders.

AD 41 – Caligula was murdered. The Praetorian Guard acclaimed Claudius princeps.

AD 50 – Claudius adopted the son of his wife Agrippina, Nero.

AD 54 – Claudius was poisoned by Agrippina and died. Nero succeeded him.

AD 55 – Claudius's son Britannicus was poisoned and died.

AD 64 – Great Fire of Rome.

AD 65 – A major conspiracy against Nero.

AD 68 – Nero was declared the enemy of the state and died. Galba became the ruler of Rome.

AD 69 – Galba was killed by the Praetorian Guard. Otho became the emperor of Rome, got defeated by Vitellius, who replaced him as emperor. Vitellius was executed. Vespasian became the emperor of Rome.

AD 79 – Vespasian died, succeeded by his son Titus. The eruption of Mount, the cities of Pompeii and Herculaneum destroyed.

AD 80 – Another fire in Rome. The Colosseum was completed.

AD 81 – Titus died. Domitian became the emperor.

AD 96 – Domitian was killed. Nerva succeeded him.

AD 97 – Nerva adopted Trajan.

AD 98 – Nerva died, succeeded by Trajan.

117 - Trajan died. Hadrian came to power.

122 - The construction of Hadrian's Wall at the northern border of Britain began.

138 - Hadrian adopted Antoninus Pius, on the condition that he in turn adopt Marcus Aurelius and Lucius Verus. Hadrian died, and was succeeded by Antoninus.

161 - Antoninus died. Marcus and Lucius Verus declared co-emperors.

169 - Lucius Verus died of plague, leaving Marcus the sole ruler of Rome.

177 - Marcus named his natural son Commodus his co-emperor.

180 - Marcus died.

192 - Commodus was strangled to death.

193 - Pertinax and, Didius Julianus were successively acclaimed emperors and, in the same year killed by the Praetorian Guard. Septimius Severus became the emperor.

198 - Septimius Severus made his eldest natural son Caracalla his co-emperor.

209 - Septimius Severus named his youngest son Publius Septimius Geta co-emperor with himself and Caracalla.

211 - Septimius Severus died. Caracalla's men killed Geta.

217 - Caracalla was killed by a member of his bodyguard. Macrinus acclaimed emperor.

218 - Elagabalus, allegedly the illegitimate son of Caracalla, captured and killed Macrinus, and became the emperor.

222 - Elagabalus was killed by the Praetorians. Severus Alexander becomes the new ruler of Rome.

235 - Severus Alexander was murdered in a mutiny. Maximinus Thrax became the ruler of Rome.

238 - Gordian I and Gordian II were declared rulers of Rome. Pupienus and Balbinus were next on throne, were murdered, and followed by Gordian III. Maximinus was killed during a mutiny.

244 - Gordian III was murdered and succeeded by Philip the Arab.

249 - Philip the Arab was killed in battle with Decius, who became the emperor. Succeeded by Hostilian, who died of plague in the same year. Gallus was next on the throne, and was followed by his son Volusianus.

253 - Gallus and Volusianus were assassinated. Aemilianus became the ruler of Rome, got killed, and was succeeded by Valerian.

260 – Valerian was captured by the Sasanian Empire. Postumus was declared ruler of Rome in the Gallic Empire.

269 – Postumus was killed by his soldiers, who in turn acclaimed one of their own, Marcus Aurelius Marius, emperor of the Gallic Empire.

275 – Aurelian was killed by the Praetorian Guard.

284 – Diocletian was proclaimed Augustus.

285 – Diocletian gave Maximian the title Caesar.

286 – Diocletian declared Maximian emperor of the West, ruling himself as emperor of the East.

293 – Diocletian established the Tetrarchy, appointing Constantius Chlorus to hold the office of Caesar under Maximian in the west and Galerius to hold the title under himself in the east.

305 – Diocletian and Maximian abdicated. Constantius and Galerius became Augusti in the West and East. Galerius appointed Flavius Valerius Severus Caesar in the West and Maximinus II Caesar in the East.

306 – Constantius died and his troops acclaimed his son Constantine the Great Emperor. Civil wars of the Tetrarchy: Rebels in Rome acclaimed Maximian's son Maxentius ruler of Rome.

308 - Civil wars of the Tetrarchy: After a failed coup against his son Maxentius, Maximian was forced to flee to Constantine's court.

310 – Maximian was forced to commit suicide.

311 – Galerius and Diocletian died. Licinius and Maximinus arranged to divide the eastern Empire between themselves.

313 – Constantine the Great and Licinius issued the Edict of Milan.

330 – Constantine the Great moved his capital to Byzantium and renamed the city Constantinople.

337 – Constantine the Great died.

379 – Theodosius I was declared the Great Augustus in the east.

380 - The Edict of Thessalonica, making Christianity the state church of the Roman Empire.

402 – The capital of the Western Roman Empire was moved to Ravenna.

410 – Sack of Rome by the Visigoths under their king Alaric I.

455 – Petronius Maximus became Augustus of the Western Roman Empire. He was killed by a crowd as he tried to escape Rome in the face of a Vandal advance. Sack of Rome by

Vandals.

476 - The Western emperor Zeno took Constantinople. The German King Odoacer took control over the West. The end of the Western Roman Empire.

Part 3: The Byzantine Empire

A Captivating Guide to Byzantium and How the Eastern Roman Empire Was Ruled by Emperors such as Constantine the Great and Justinian

Introduction

Long after the Western Roman Empire ceased to exist, another Roman Empire was alive and well. This empire was the only organized state in the Western world which persisted in the same shape from antiquity until the dawn of the modern age. Unaffected by the Dark Ages, this society was a fusion of ancient Greece, Rome, and Christianity – a fusion that grew and matured centuries before the Renaissance.

The Byzantine Empire was founded during the chaotic third century. It was the time when revolts and civil wars were common, and Roman emperors merely lasted for a year. In the midst of this turmoil, the new hierarchical, ordered world arose on the Bosphorus River. But the Eastern Roman Empire wasn't a typical autocratic society. Anyone, including humble farmers and orphaned women, had a chance to find their way onto the throne. Byzantium's greatest ruler was formerly a lowly peasant from present-day Macedonia, while one empress was an ex-courtesan.

Despite being a deeply religious society, its educational system was thorough and surprisingly secular. There were no Dark Ages in Byzantium. This part of the world was the guardian of light and civilization in Medieval Europe and beyond.[101] It presented a shield that protected the rest of Europe from rapidly expanding Islamic forces.[102] At the same time, it preserved invaluable texts and artifacts of the Greek and Latin culture – and created more. The mosaics of Ravenna were the work of Byzantine artisans, as was the Hagia Sofia. The timeless Roman law, which served as a basis and inspiration for a great majority of European legal systems was created in Constantinople, not Rome. It wasn't introduced by Octavian, Claudius, or Trajan. The name of the mighty emperor who gave us such achievement was Justinian.

Byzantine Empire was not the real name of this state. It was formally known as the Eastern Roman Empire. The citizens of Constantinople and its rulers saw themselves as Romans, not Byzantines. Not just them – their neighboring countries including their enemies saw this empire as Roman. When Constantinople fell after eleven centuries, the Ottoman sultan Mehmed II took the title Caesar of Rome. It wasn't until eighteenth century that the scholars of the west denied the Eastern Empire the tag "Roman." Byzantium – the name of a tiny town which served as a basis of Constantinople – has become the official name of this state centuries after it collapsed.

The Eastern and Western world were loosely linked by Christianity until 1054 when the church split into Catholic and Orthodox halves. The hostility culminated during the Crusades. The Eastern Empire never fully recovered from the violent assaults from the Catholic West. It lost the capacity to resist the Ottomans' invasion. When it fell, it was quickly forgotten. Out of sheer ignorance, its new name, Byzantine, became the synonym for obscurity and even deviousness.

The history of the Byzantine Empire is a lesser known one, yet it is among the most captivating. This book is a story of power and glory, anarchy and order, paganism and Christianity, war and peace, the West and the East. You'll get familiar with the roots of the greatest controversies that defined the history of Europe and the entirety of Western civilization – the conflict between the Catholic and Orthodox churches, and the one between Christianity and Islam. You'll read the stories of remarkable emperors you've never heard of and about the astonishing bravery of Graeco-Roman heroes such as Constantine Dragases, who resisted the Ottomans until the end, and Belisarius, who fought the Persians to reconquer what used to be the Western Empire.

The story of Constantinople began in 324 AD when Constantine decided – or was told by a divine voice, as the ancient legend says – to establish the new capital of the world on a hill upon the Bosphorus. Europe was still Roman, but the city of Rome was not as important. It belonged to the past, just like the ancient city of Troy. Byzantium was the future – a very promising and dynamic one, as we will see in the following pages.

The Western Empire continued to exist in some form for another century and a half after Constantinople was built. The two empires lived simultaneously, and a few rulers managed to reunite them occasionally, but only for a brief couple of years or so until one day, the barbaric King Odoacer took the West and sent the Western imperial regalia to the Eastern emperor.

Our story begins with the period called Late Roman Empire, which started with Diocletian and was profoundly influenced by Constantine the Great. The first three chapters cover the struggle of the two halves of the Roman world, the ways their emperors tried to resist enemies outside and within the borders until the final fall of Rome. The rest of the book addresses the Roman "future," the new world that was just as mighty as Augustan Rome, and the most glorious (and equally controversial) figures of the "New Rome" – the Byzantine Emperor Justinian and Empress Theodora.

Chapter 1 – Laying the Foundation for the Byzantine Empire

Constantine's vision and energy were remarkable, but the founding of the new Roman capital would be impossible if it weren't for Diocletian and his profound reforms. He brought changes that affected almost every aspect of Roman society. Some of them were popular, others were not, but he certainly knew what he was doing.

The third century was a time of tremendous suffering for the Roman people. The days of stability and glory were over. Armies fought each other within the Empire, while barbarian hordes attacked the frontiers. The populace was drowning in debt and ever-increasing taxes. Twenty-nine emperors tried to establish new dynasties. All of them ended up murdered, more often by the Praetorian Guard than by outside forces – all but one.

How Diocletian Changed Rome Forever

Diocletian was a soldier from Dalmatia (in present-day Croatia). He gained power in the same way as the others: by killing his predecessor and defeating his army. But he did everything else differently. He knew that the Roman Empire was too vast and complex to be controlled by a single man. Unblinded by power, he decided to share it. He made Maximian, his old drinking buddy, a co-emperor and divided the empire in half.[103] Diocletian took control over the eastern (richer, more-cultured, and mainly Greek) half of the empire and gave his friend the western, Latin part. It all worked so well that Diocletian decided to divide the empire even further, appoint two junior emperors and establishing the tetrarchy. Officially, there was still one, unique Roman Empire. The four men had the power to lead armies and issue laws. The system was efficient, at least temporarily. Borders and provinces were under control, and Diocletian turned to other issues. He reformed the administration and made the tax system more efficient. Finally, he rebranded the institution of the Emperor of Rome. Hiding behind the symbols of the obsolete republic, which worked so well for Octavian Augustus and his descendants, was no longer appropriate. The days of the principate were over.[104] The emperor was no longer the "first among equals." Diocletian elevated himself from the masses and was thereafter presented as the embodiment of Jupiter on Earth. Unlike the emperors from the previous epochs who used to be depicted either in togas or military uniforms, Diocletian was dressed in a golden robe and wore a crown. It was the beginning of the Dominate, or the late Roman Empire.[105]

Romans had deified their deceased emperors for centuries. As most of the populace were pagans, they easily accepted the idea of another divine ruler. But not all of them were pagans. People all throughout the empire had embraced a new religion that gave them hope against arbitrary injustice. Christianity gave them faith in an all-powerful, yet loving God who would punish the wicked and reward the just with eternal life. And the growing number of Christians in the empire weren't willing to swallow Diocletian's claims of divinity.

Christians were model citizens. They paid their taxes without complaining and were willing to serve in the army. But there was something that Diocletian couldn't tolerate. Christians undermined the essence of his imperial authority by refusing to make a sacrifice to the emperor. They insisted that there was only one God and highlighted the fact that the emperor, no matter how powerful, was just a man.

So Diocletian decided to wipe them out. Numerous churches were destroyed, and holy writings were burned. People were captured, some of them even killed, but Christianity persisted. All that repression just made it stronger. The pagans sympathized with their Christian neighbors, rejecting Diocletian's propaganda, which depicted them as immoral, godless, dangerous dissidents, and even cannibals. In reality, Christians were common people who paid taxes, had stable families, and were honest in trade. Everyone knew that. Diocletian's battle against Christianity turned against him. Finally, in 305 AD, Diocletian abdicated. Maximian, who ruled the West, had to abdicate too. Their junior emperors (Caesars), Galerius and Constantinus the Pale, had now become emperors and were requested to name their own respective Caesars. Everything went smoothly, except for one thing. Some of the tetrarchs (tetrarchy was the rule of four) had sons. Those sons weren't the least bit happy when they found out that some other men were made heirs to their fathers. The perfect order that Diocletian established had already started to melt.

The sons of Maximian and Constantinus the Pale, Maxentius, and Constantine, believed they were to become the heirs to the throne. When they discovered they were left with nothing, like ordinary private citizens, they felt betrayed. And of course, they did not accept it.

The Rise of Constantine

Unlike other tetrarchs, Constantinus the Pale was honest and down-to-earth. He never persecuted Christians or anyone else. His army – even the highest ranks – included people of all religions. Naturally, he was extremely popular with the army. But unfortunately, he was seriously ill. He wasn't 'pale' metaphorically; he was dying of leukemia. This had become clear during his campaign in Britain in early 306. He succumbed to his illness on July 25, 306. The army was informed that his junior emperor named Severus – whom most of them had never heard of – would take Constantinus' place.

Constantine often joined his father in campaigns and was there when he died. The army was loyal to him just as it was to Constantinus. So, they declared Constantine their emperor, and another civil war had begun.

Meanwhile, encouraged by the way Constantine claimed power, Maximian's son, Maxentius, seized Rome. Now there were six men claiming to be the emperors of Rome – the four 'legal' (following the system of succession established by Diocletian) tetrarchs, and two 'illegal' ones (who seized power by force) – Constantine and Maxentius. By 312, only the two intruders were left in the West. Then Constantine, with his forty thousand men, invaded Maxentius' Italy.

Unlike Constantine, Maxentius was a cruel and largely unpopular ruler. He wasn't assured that his army would defend him from Constantine, so he escaped the city. The two armies soon met at the Milvian Bridge. Constantine, who later claimed he was guided by Christ, crushed Maxentius' forces. The next day, Constantine triumphantly entered Rome holding Maxentius' head on a spear. He had become the sole ruler of the Western Roman Empire. But back in the fourth century, the West was not the best. It was just the beginning for Constantine.

The bust of Constantine the Great[106]

katie chao and ben muessig, CC BY-SA 2.0 <https://creativecommons.org/licenses/by-sa/2.0>, via Wikimedia Commons
https://commons.wikimedia.org/wiki/File:MMA_bust_02.jpg

Chapter 2 – The Age of Constantine

Constantine marched into Rome as a liberator who set his people free from the ruthless tyrant. The Senate hailed him enthusiastically when he entered the Forum. But then he did something unthinkable, something that no Roman Emperor had ever done in history - he refused to offer the customary sacrifice to the ancient deity of victory. He had won his victory against Maxentius wielding the cross and the sword, and with the help of the Christian God. This was a turning point in Roman history and the one that linked the Roman Empire and the Christian church forever.

His impact on Christianity was enormous, but Constantine had still not become a genuine Christian.[107] He never renounced his title of Pontifex Maximus, and the depictions of his favorite pagan deities, Sol Invictus and Mars Conservator, still appeared on his coins. It is questionable whether he even understood the deeper meaning of Christianity and the theological concept of resurrection. Nevertheless, he was wise enough to realize that Christianity did not have to be seen as a threat to the establishment. He saw the new religion as an opportunity to prove himself as a just ruler and to unite the people within the Empire. So, he stopped all persecutions of Christians, and in 313 legalized the faith by issuing an edict of toleration. From that point on, Christianity took another purpose: to support Constantine's regime the way paganism supported Diocletian's. But he made sure not to alienate the pagans, who still made up the majority of the populace, and he still had not made the new religion the exclusive one of the empire.

Conquering the East

While Constantine was portraying himself as a model of religious toleration in the West, the East had fallen into the hands of Emperor Licinus. Licinus had gotten rid of the competition in his half of the empire, but he was afraid of Constantine. Assured that the Christians would support his western rival, he started persecuting them the way Diocletian did. Constantine saw his opportunity and came with his army. After a couple of weeks, the armies of the two Roman emperors met near the ancient Greek colony of Byzantium – which was to become the center of the known universe – where on September 18, 324, Constantine's forces completely devastated Licinus'. Constantine the Greatest, as he named himself after his triumph over Maximinus, had now become Constantine the Victor, the sole emperor of the Roman Empire.

Once again, Constantine emerged as the protector of the people. He came and saved the Christians without persecuting the pagan populace. He was carefully maintaining the guise of tolerance and neutrality until he managed to eliminate the last of his rivals. Now that he had become the sole ruler, he could embrace Christianity more openly. His mother, Helena – the world's first pilgrim – went to the Holy Land and founded numerous hostels and hospitals along the way, including the Church of the Nativity in Bethlehem, and the Church of the Holy Sepulchre at Golgotha in Jerusalem at the exact spot where Christ had been crucified, and where Hadrian later built the temple of Venus – which apparently had to be demolished.

The Church of the Holy Sepulchre, also called the Basilica of the Holy Sepulchre, or the Church of the Resurrection[108]
Jorge Láscar from Australia, CC BY 2.0 <https://creativecommons.org/licenses/by/2.0>, via Wikimedia Commons
https://commons.wikimedia.org/wiki/File:Jerusalem_The_Church_of_the_Holy_Sepulchre,_the_place_where_Jesus_was_crucified_(and_su pposedly,_buried)_(10350972756).jpg

This was a time of rapid change within the empire, which left far-reaching consequences. Constantine carried out a number of reforms to stabilize the shaken empire. Markets and commerce recovered, and the working classes started working again (instead of fighting in civil wars). The peasant farmers were obliged to stay on their land. The members of guilds, as well of their children, had to stay in their occupations. These changes eventually resulted in the feudal system that was common throughout the West. In the stable and prosperous East, however, these reforms had little effect.[109]

As the material well-being improved throughout the empire, Constantine went further in nurturing Christianity. He banned pagan sacrifices and ritual orgies, put an end to the practice of crucifixion and the violent gladiatorial games (chariot races persisted as less violent), and confiscated temple treasuries to build churches.

The united Roman Empire and Christianity were linked for good, but then a new challenge arose. A young priest (and brilliant speaker) from Egypt called Arius started teaching that Christ was just not truly a god and that he was inferior to God the Father. This heresy threatened to tear the still decentralized and disorganized church apart. So, Constantine decided to put an end to the chaos and, when his idea of 'working the differences out and living in harmony' failed, he announced a great council. On May 20, 325, in Nicaea, Constantine gathered all bishops in the empire and proposed a simple solution to the complex theological issue of the nature of Christ. The Arians did not dare to disagree with the emperor, and Arius himself was condemned afterward. Constantine restored Christian unity just as he had done with the empire.

A Fresh Start: The New Capital of the Roman Empire

Now that Constantine had set everything up, he made a massive basilica in Rome, with a huge statue of himself inside, and several other churches, including one for the pope. But he preferred to live in another city and create a fresh start for the profoundly changed empire. A divine voice, as he later claimed, showed him the site where he should build New Rome (Nova Roma).

The thousand years old Greek colony called Byzantium was placed on a perfect spot between the eastern and western borders of the empire. Surrounded on three sides with water, it had incredible natural defenses. The city possessed a large harbor at the center of the lucrative trade routes between the Mediterranean and the Black Sea. Last but not least, this was the site where Constantine crushed Licinus and became the empire's sole ruler.

New Rome was built remarkably quickly in just six years. People from all parts of the empire were happy to move there and enjoy the numerous benefits, including free grain and fresh water, as well as prospects of advancement on the social ladder. The new capital was dedicated on May 11, 330, and was thereafter known as Constantinople.

The Last Years of Constantine the Great: A Dark Secret, Baptism, and Death

In his later years, Constantine struggled to preserve the political and religious harmony. He ruled oppressively and utilized severe measures to return some prosperity. He was successful in doing so, but he was also becoming increasingly ruthless. He couldn't tolerate any prospective rival and he had already killed many, but this time it was different. There was a man whom the masses loved so much and whom they wanted to see as the next emperor. This man was named Crispus, Constantine's oldest son. The emperor couldn't stand his son's popularity. He accused Crispus of attempting to seduce his stepmother, Fausta, and had both of them killed.

Despite his firm hand, Constantine couldn't control everything. He wasn't able to manage the church the way he wanted. He influenced the official doctrine established in Nicaea, but the minds and faith of ordinary people were beyond his power. Heretics such as Arius gained the support of many, even though they'd previously been banished from the church. Constantine was never sure which faction within the church was right and was always interested in supporting the one that was stronger and more popular. In the end, he was baptized by the Arian bishop called Eusebius. Trying to fortify his position, Constantine was again after military glory. In 337, he went to attack the Persians, but couldn't make it. He was too sick to fight this battle. Aware that he was dying, he needed the last-minute blessing. The emperor who had such a great impact on history by embracing Christianity was baptized just before his death.[110] He was buried as an "equal of the apostles" in the lavish Church of the Holy Apostles in Constantinople.

Chapter 3 – From Constantine's Death to the Fall of the Western Empire

Even though the empire had been deeply transformed during the reigns of Domitian and Constantine, the citizens of both the West and East continued to identify themselves as Romans. Some of them were Christians, but paganism persisted too. The temples of the old state religion were full, as were the churches. Christianity was legal, but it still hadn't become the official faith of the empire. But that was not the only issue that Constantine left unsolved.

The late emperor didn't care who would succeed him as long as (as we've seen in the previous chapter) no one tried to replace him while he was still alive. Now that he died, his three sons - Constantine II, Constantius II, and Constans - divided the empire among themselves, but soon after, they started killing each other in order to take the whole. At the same time, Constantius II, who was the most capable of the brothers, managed to get rid of anyone who might claim to have a drop of his father's blood, with the exception of a younger cousin called Julian, who didn't seem to be much of a threat. Then, after three years, Constantius II invaded the area controlled by his youngest brother, and another period of civil war had begun.

Julian the Apostate: Zeus Strikes Back

The little Julian (Flavius Claudius Julianus, later known as Julian the Apostate), who was only five years old when his older cousins were busy fighting each other, spent his early years under a kind of house arrest. Even when he grew up, he displayed no imperial ambitions. Julian used to read the Greek and Roman classics as a child, and when he turned nineteen, he managed to get permission to travel and pursue his studies of the classical world. He traveled from Pergamum to Ephesus, learned philosophy, secretly rejected Christianity, and embraced Neoplatonism – a school of thought based on Plotinus' interpretation of Platonic philosophy. Julian was careful to keep his apostasy hidden, and he appeared to his Christian teachers as the most pious of men. But the day had come when he no longer could proceed with his life of a scholar. The emperor needed him.

Meanwhile, Constantius II managed to get rid of his brothers and take the whole empire. But Rome had so many enemies, and it was too challenging for a single ruler to manage everything. Barbarians were invading northern territories, but he needed to fight against Persia. Ironically, now all his brothers had been killed, he desperately needed someone of his blood to take care of other fronts. So, he called for Julian, gave him the rank of Caesar (junior emperor), gave him 360 utterly incapable men (who "knew only how to pray"[111]), and sent him to Gaul.

Julian was an introverted scholar, and he had zero military experience. No one really expected he would achieve anything, but they were wrong. During the five years he spent in Gaul, he managed to organize the local army, expel the barbarians, set twenty thousand prisoners free, brought peace to the province, defeated the Germanic tribes in their own territory, took his king as the prisoner of war, and sent him to Constantinople in chains.

Constantius felt threatened by his young cousin's victory and instantly demanded money and troops from Gaul to be sent to him as a support against the Persians. Julian's men did not want to leave their families and go to the east, so they mutinied. The soldiers gathered overnight, surrounded Julian's palace, hailed him as Augustus, and demanded him to lead them against Constantius. Having received a sign from Zeus (as he claimed), Julian accepted, and another war nearly began. Since he no longer needed to pretend he was Christian, Julian sent manifestos to all important cities in order to restore Roman traditional religion. But then the news spread that Constantius died of an illness. Julian arrived in Constantinople, where he was welcomed enthusiastically by the crowds as well as the Senate.

But Julian wasn't happy. He saw decay, greed, and a lack of discipline everywhere. The empire was sick, and he blamed Christianity – with its 'feminine' attributes of kindness and forgiveness that replaced the traditional Roman sense of honor and duty – as the major cause of this decay.

Julian was smart enough to realize that persecution wouldn't work, so he published an edict of toleration. But at the same time, he proclaimed traditional Roman paganism as a superior religion. He reopened temples throughout the empire and tried several subtle measures – and some less subtle ones – to persuade the populace to return to the old religion, but without success. Then he came to the idea to enforce his ideas by a great military victory, just as Constantine had done by winning the battle of the Milvian Bridge.

Julian the Apostate[112]
Classical Numismatic Group, Inc. http://www.cngcoins.com, CC BY-SA 2.5 <https://creativecommons.org/licenses/by-sa/2.5>, via Wikimedia Commons https://commons.wikimedia.org/wiki/File:IVLIANVS.gif

Determined to destroy Christianity, Julian sent messengers to ask the oracle at Delphi for a prophecy. The answer was not what he hoped for. The words of the oracle were: "Tell the emperor that my hall has fallen to the ground. Phoibos no longer has his house, nor his mantic bay, nor his prophetic spring; the water has dried up."[113]

We'll never know for sure whether this prophecy was authentic, or if it was all made up by contemporary Christians, but it wasn't the only sign that things would not end up well for Julian. He ordered the rebuilding of the ancient Jewish temple in Jerusalem just to prove that Christ was wrong when he prophesied that the temple wouldn't be restored until the end times. But the works were interrupted twice – once by an earthquake and the second time by the fire that burned the entire structure to the ground. As if this wasn't enough, the emperor was becoming increasingly unpopular day after day, especially after he closed a Christian cathedral and used the gold to pay his army. Nevertheless, he wasn't willing to give up.

In the spring of 363, he marched east to attack Persia. His army was a proper Roman army, huge and powerful, and it easily entered the Persian territory. But the Persian capital of Ctesiphon was surrounded by high walls. They couldn't break in, but they also couldn't stay around. The heat was unbearable for the Romans, and the news emerged that a large Persian army was coming, so Julian reluctantly abandoned the siege. A few months later, the Persians attacked, and Julian instantly got a fatal wound. Julian was the last pagan Roman Emperor and the attempts to restore the ancient world ended with him. He was also the last emperor from the Constantinian dynasty, and now the path was open for a new line.

Further Decay: Valentinian, Valens, and Gratian

The world continued to change, and the Roman Empire was soon flooded by Germanic tribes who came not as invaders, but as settlers who wanted to take refuge from the Huns – the new force that frightened even them. Nevertheless, they weren't willing to assimilate and accept the Roman culture, and the social patterns changed. At the same time, the empire was ruled by one incompetent emperor after another.[114] The first that came after Julian managed to suffocate himself by leaving a brazier burning in his tent overnight. His successors, Valentinian and Valens, divided the empire again. Valentinian ruled the West for eleven years before he died, leaving a son named Gratian as his heir. Gratian was too young and he fell under the influence of his uncle.

Valens made a deal with the two hundred thousand Visigoths and Ostrogoths who wanted to settle in the Roman territory. The newcomers would be given land in Thrace, and they would provide troops. But it did not end well. Great tensions between the locals and the newcomers escalated and, in 378, Valens and Gratian jointly (but without an accurate report or a proper plan) attacked the Goths near Adrianople. The Romans were exhausted from the long march and tortured by heat, and the Goths slaughtered two-thirds of them. This was a catastrophe that allowed every barbaric tribe to enter the empire and do whatever they pleased – and so they did. The Goths even spread east and threatened Constantinople. The situation was almost impossible to handle.

Theodosius to the Rescue

Now that Valens was dead, the western emperor, Gratian, appointed his best general, Theodosius, as the emperor of the eastern half of the empire. Tens of thousands of experienced soldiers had been killed at the Adrianople disaster, and Theodosius had to find some fresh blood quickly. He pressed virtually everyone into service, and finally let the barbarian troops in. He basically confirmed the arrangement made by Valens, but he did it smarter, paying more attention to the details. It worked at the moment, although it left disastrous consequences that would become visible within a generation: the fall of Rome and the beginning of the Dark Ages on the Western Roman Empire.

In 382, on his way to Thessalonica, Theodosius fell ill and looked as though he would die. Like Constantine, he wanted to wash his hands and be baptized before the end of his life. However, after the baptism, he recovered. This brought a deep change to the way he ruled the empire. He no longer could kill innocents or ignore the issues within the church. He dealt with the Arian heresy and, soon after, with paganism within the empire. Prompted by his religious mentor, Bishop Ambrose of Milan, Theodosius finally closed the public temples and renounced the title of Pontifex Maximus – the chief priest of the traditional Roman religion – previously held by all Roman Emperors since Augustus. He wasn't really willing to do so but was forced to. After killing a few thousand civilians to suppress a mutiny in Thessalonica, Ambrose did not allow Theodosius to enter the Church until he made atonement. It took him months, but eventually, Theodosius apologized and performed penance.

Quickly after, he put an end to all things pagan, from the Olympic Games, to the Delphic Oracle and the Temple of Vesta. The vestal virgins were dismissed, and the eternal fire extinguished. In 391, Theodosius officially made Christianity – which had also evolved and accepted some Roman features by this point – the only religion in the empire.

The Sack of Rome

Theodosius' successors weren't strong enough to deal with the 'barbaric' elements in the empire, and Germanic and other tribes achieved enormous power. The people who controlled armies had more influence than the emperors of the East and the West. Rome was under the command of a general of Vandal origin called Stilicho, even though there was an emperor (Honorius), too. It was actually rather convenient, because Stilicho was a brilliant commander, able to put down revolts and invasions of Germanic barbarians. But, unfortunately, neither the Senate in Rome, nor the public officials in Constantinople supported him. When he tried to bribe the Visigothic King Alaric instead of fighting him (which was a reasonable decision that could save many Roman lives and postpone a catastrophe), the Emperor Honorius was persuaded that Stilicho had betrayed Rome. The mighty general was killed, and Italy was defenseless. So, in 401, Alaric's army invaded Italy. The Goths climbed the Seven Hills of Rome and ruined the city. Honorius escaped to Ravena, and the citizens of both Rome and the western provinces, such as Britania, were left to fend for themselves.

The Huns

Constantinople was still safe. The Eastern Empire kept the universal and divine entitlements of the empire. As for the West, it was doomed. Alarmed by the sack of Rome, the new Eastern Emperor, Theodosius II, ordered massive walls constructed around Constantinople. Alaric died soon after and did not pose a threat anymore, but those walls served the Eastern Emperors well for another thousand years. In fact, they immediately proved very useful. Meanwhile, a new horrifying threat came from Asia – Attila and the Huns. The Huns gave a new meaning to the word "uncivilized." They slept on their horses, never changed clothes, never bathed or cooked their food. They were so terrifying that people throughout the empire called Attila "The Scourge of God."

Constantinople was forced to let the Huns enter the Roman territory and to give Attila enormous riches to leave them alone. But a few months later they came back because of curious circumstances. The emperor's sister, Honoria, tried her best to escape a forced marriage with a senator. When all her previous attempts failed, she sent a letter and a ring to Attila, who then came to take what was his.

There was no one left in Rome to resist Attila or try to persuade him to spare the city – except for Pope Leo. The two men met and talked, and the Huns left the city. The next morning, Attila was found dead in his tent.

The Final Fall of the Western Empire and the Resilience of the East

Attila died, and the Huns no longer threatened the Roman Empire, but the true enemy was still there, and it was not only integrated into the society, but effectively controlled it. The barbarians were just behind the throne, exercising power and controlling the emperors. When Emperor Valentinian III decided to get rid of his barbarian master, he was killed too. His widow asked the Vandals to come and help Romans. They came, sacked Rome, and took the empress with themselves to Carthage.

At the same time, Constantinople was under control of the Sarmatian General, Aspar, and his puppet-emperor, named Leo. But Leo wasn't happy with his status and was seeking the way to overthrow his master – but not the way Valentinian did in the West. Instead, he found a way to take the military control from him. With the help of the Isaurian General, Tarasicodissa, he managed to charge Aspar with treason. In turn, Tarasicodissa – now Hellenized and renamed Zeno – was given the hand of Leo's daughter and the power needed to resist Aspar.

Meanwhile, Leo decided to subjugate the Vandal kingdom of North Africa, and he used all available resources to equip the army. However, the commander in charge was the worst possible choice – his brother-in-law, called Basiliscus, who landed away from Carthage, accidentally wrecked the fleet, destroyed the army, panicked, and ran away.

Leo was succeeded by Zeno in 474, but Basiliscus and his sister, Verina, soon overthrew him, and the disgraceful commander took over the throne. He soon proved that his ability to rule was on par with his ability to lead an army. His actions provoked massive rebellion. Then Zeno returned with an army. Basiliscus' generals gladly switched sides, and so did the Senate.

While Zeno was busy reestablishing stability in the Eastern Roman Empire, the West was collapsing. In 476, a barbarian general, Odoacer, sent the teenage Emperor Romulus Augustulus into exile. Odoacer then took the crown and scepter and sent them to Zeno. The Eastern Emperor wasn't willing to support the barbaric general in taking the West, but he couldn't fight him either. Eventually, he came up with a great plan; he gave the Ostrogothic King Theodoric (who at the time was making a mess in the Balkans) authority to rule the West. The Goths overwhelmed Odoacer and settled in Italy. At the same time, the Eastern Empire finally became free from any internal barbaric influence. Zeno managed to restore stability but didn't manage to live long enough to see the new era that started thanks to his effort.

Chapter 4 – The Age of Justinian, the Greatest Ruler of the Byzantine Empire

Zeno's immediate successor was Anastasius I, who established some new, sustainable patterns of government, bureaucracy, and economic development in the Eastern Empire, reformed the taxation system, introduced a new currency, minimized corruption, and left a considerable budget surplus. He died childless and, in 518, an unlikely heir came to the throne. Justin came from a peasant family from Thrace, joined the army in Constantinople, and rose to the position of commander of the palace guard. Now, with the support of the military (encouraged by donations in silver), he became the emperor. Justin was 70 at the time and wasn't properly educated to run a state, but his nephew and adopted son, Peter Sabbatius, was both fairly young (36) and well educated. Peter was grateful for all the support he received from his uncle, which included the finest education available, and he changed his name to Justinian.

Aware of his power as the emperor's adopted son, Justinian was enthusiastic about adopting a more aggressive foreign policy. His two major goals were to retake the West and liberate Rome from the barbarians and to restore the relations with papacy and reunite the church. The news disturbed the Gothic king in Italy, who knew his rule was crumbling. However, Justinian wasn't in a hurry. He spent many days watching the chariot races at the Hippodrome, where he, unlike the rulers before him, openly supported "the Blues" against "the Greens." His hobby allowed him to connect with the vast network of citizens supporting the same team, and so he knew better than anyone else what was going on in the city on all levels. Those people gave him much valuable information, and more: they introduced him to a beautiful young actress (the word "actress" was a synonym for "prostitute" back then) named Theodora. He fell madly in love with her and, despite her status of "a lady of the stage," married her with the consent of his benevolent uncle emperor.

Justin was still the emperor, but it was Justinian who made all decisions. He offered support to the neighboring peoples that struggled under the tyrannies of their masters. The emissaries from around the region gathered in Constantinople. The city virtually became the center of the world. The vassal kings loyal to the king of Persia quickly changed sides, encouraged by the support from Constantinople. Moreover, a Byzantine army led by Justinian's bodyguard called Belisarius invaded Persian Armenia. This was just the first in the line of expansionistic actions that were soon to take place.

The Coronation of Justinian and Theodora

In 527, now seriously ill, Justin, prompted by the Senate, crowned Justinian as co-emperor. By the end of the year, Justin was dead and the empire belonged to Justinian and Theodora. They were so much different from anyone who had ever been on the throne of the Roman Empire. The coronation in Hagia Sofia was luxurious, and it anticipated a new age of glory.

Justinian believed the Roman Empire was not complete without Rome. There was one God in heaven, and there should also be only one empire on earth. Since he was the emperor, it was his responsibility to restore the heavenly order and bring those western territories back.

Justinian I the Great[115]
Petar Milošević, CC BY-SA 4.0 <https://creativecommons.org/licenses/by-sa/4.0>, via Wikimedia Commons
https://commons.wikimedia.org/wiki/File:Mosaic_of_Justinianus_I_-_Basilica_San_Vitale_(Ravenna).jpg

The Roman Law

Although admired for his imperial goals and actions, Justinian wasn't really popular. His politics included costly military actions and construction projects, and it all came from taxes. Even the rich and privileged could not continue to escape their commitments, which increased the hostility between the nobility and the emperor. Justinian favored pragmatic individuals over blue-blooded ones and surrounded himself with a few extremely capable men. One of them was Tribonian, an amazing lawyer who knew Roman laws and edicts more than anyone else in the empire.

At the time, Roman law was a mess. Even though everything was simple at the dawn of civilization, things had seriously changed over the last thousand years, which brought numerous contradictory precedents, conflicting interpretations, and special exemptions. None of them were written down in any one place. So, Julian decided to systematize the Roman Law, remove repetitions and inconsistencies, and create a comprehensive legal code – the first one in imperial history. Tribonian made it happen; he produced the codex that was to become the basis of most legal system that we still use today.[116]

Belisarius, the Superior General

In 528, the Persians attacked again, this time with a large, intimidating army. The Byzantine forces led by General Belisarius not only defeated them, but also took part of Armenia. War had finally broken out with Persia, and he had been busy reorganizing the eastern army. The aging Persian king sent a huge army to flatten the Romans, but Belisarius defeated it with his characteristic flair, and he even managed to conquer part of Persian Armenia. Almost at the same time, the Vandals in North Africa overthrew their king, who was at least formally a loyal vassal to Constantinople, and sent some offensive threats. Shortly after that, Belisarius was free to deal with them too. But something unexpected was happening in Constantinople.

The Nika Revolt

While Justinian was contemplating reconquering the Roman territories, Constantinople was at the edge of revolt. High taxes and corrupt officials made the mobs angry, but there was the drop that spilled the glass. The Blues and the Greens occasionally caused incidents – pretty much like today's football hooligans tend to do – and Justinian restricted their privileges. Then, during the ides of January, someone from the crowd started cursing Justinian. The emperor responded harshly and made the crowd furious, forcing him to retreat to the palace. When the Hippodrome was open for new games three days later, thirty thousand people started screaming *"Níka!"* ("Conquer!"). Justinian had to flee again, and the masses went out to the streets, broke into prisons, and then the convicts joined them too.

The imperial police were unable to deal with the situation. The aristocrats were eager to see the emperor overthrown, and they gave the rioters the weapons. The city was in flames. The emperor's advisers advised him to escape while he still could, but the empress raised her voice and disagreed, stating that an emperor cannot allow himself to become a fugitive.[117] Then the solution emerged. Belisarius had just returned from Persia and was still not sent to Africa. He was able to take care of Constantinople. The mighty general took his men and went to the streets. The great majority of rioters were gathered at the Hippodrome, where the army entered and killed them all. Thirty thousand men were dead, and the city went deadly quiet.

In the aftermath, nineteen senators who supported the rioters were killed and thrown into the sea. No one ever dared again to cause Justinian any trouble.

The Byzantine Golden Age

The disaster at the Hippodrome was also an opportunity. Justinian began a large building program which transformed the city into a truly magnificent metropolis. An extravagant new Senate building replaced the burned one. A huge subterranean cistern was built to provide fresh water to the people as well as the numerous fountains. The most important building that had been demolished in the rebellion was the Hagia Sophia. The church was built by Constantius II and rebuilt by Theodosius II. Justinian abandoned the old project and made perhaps the most impressive cathedral ever built.

Hagia Sophia today (adapted into a mosque), Istanbul, Turkey[118]
Arild Vågen, CC BY-SA 3.0 <https://creativecommons.org/licenses/by-sa/3.0>, via Wikimedia Commons
https://commons.wikimedia.org/wiki/File:Hagia_Sophia_Mars_2013.jpg

Belisarius Retakes the Provinces

After the domestic peace was reestablished and the construction works almost complete, Justinian focused on his dreams of imperial expansion. He sent Belisarius to Africa, but he did not spend too much on the campaign. Belisarius had only eighteen thousand men and essential supplies. Nevertheless, the able general managed to defeat the Vandals in Africa, mostly thanks to remarkable discipline. Carthage was reconquered and once again Roman.

Justinian granted his favorite general a triumph and immediately sent him to Sicily. At the same time, another general was sent to northern Italy. Belisarius triumphed, but the other general who was to support him from the north unfortunately failed, was killed, forcing the headless army to withdraw. But the next year, Belisarius entered Rome. His achievement was incredible, but he only had five thousand men. After a few dramatic actions, he wrote to Justinian asking for more men. However, his plea for reinforcements was interpreted as an intention of Belisarius to take the throne. He was only sent a few thousand men and still, in only five years he subdued thousands and returned Africa and Italy to the empire. He might have been able to retake Spain and most of Western Europe if it wasn't for the empress who believed that the general was too powerful to be trusted.

The Hard Times: the Plague

When Justinian finally sent reinforcements to Belisarius, it consisted of seven thousand men led by an elderly general named Narsus. Narsus was an influential figure himself, and he seriously undermined Belisarius' authority. The already small army split in half. The part of army led by Belisarius entered Milan, but was required to return to the Eastern Empire and fight the Persians. When this campaign ended, there was no need for further war. All the enemies, including the Vandals and the Goths, were crippled. The Byzantine Empire was mightier than ever, but the period of prosperity was short-lived. A new and much different enemy emerged. Rats carrying fleas infected with plague came to Egypt, the major source of imperial grain, and the disease spread throughout the empire. In Constantinople, ten thousand people a day died for a period of four months. When the plague finally ended, the populace had to face famine and poverty.

When the disease raged throughout the empire, Belisarius was safe on the Persian frontier. But Justinian was stricken by the disease. Theodora was afraid that Belisarius would take the throne if Justinian died, and she utilized her power to banish the general in disgrace, accusing him of treason.

The Persians took the opportunity to attack the weakened empire, but they only managed to end up infected. At the same time, the Goths seized Italy once again, and there was no Belisarius to resist them. Meanwhile, Justinian recovered, called for Belisarius, and sent him to Italy once again, followed by only four thousand men, only to discover that the people in Italy do not want to pay taxes to the impoverished empire. Justinian was out of options.

Shortly after, Theodora died. Justinian called Belisarius back, gave him a luxurious palace, and built a statue in his honor. Then he sent the general Narses – who had previously undermined Belisarius' authority in Italy – with a large army to claim victory in Rome, and another, Liberius, to retake Spain.

However, Justinian's imperial plans had to be suspended. The plague returned, followed by an earthquake. The impoverished state and drastically reduced number of men that were able to serve the army were not sufficient to protect the frontiers. Soon the Huns started entering the Byzantine territory, and only Constantinople was safe thanks to its walls and natural defenses. Luckily, Justinian still had Belisarius, who was equally brilliant as he had been previously. The general led a few hundred guards and veterans, crushed the Huns, and expelled them from the territory. But he also inspired jealousy in his emperor, who suddenly fired Belisarius and took command of the army.

Eventually, Justinian managed to bring Rome back and maintain peace until the end of his life and reign. He was the last Roman Emperor to speak Latin as his first language, and one of the greatest visionaries the empire ever had.[119]

Chapter 5 – Heraclius

The emperors who, successively, came after Justinian – Justin II, Tiberius II Constantine, Maurice, and Phocas – are hardly worth mentioning. The West was lost again – this time forever – and the East lived its life more or less the same way it did before. Businesses were thriving, merchants were traveling the roads built by previous emperors, and students were learning at the universities. Even the lower classes were somewhat relaxed during the time of peace, which unfortunately did not last.

In the sixth century, wars and disasters made life difficult for everyone, especially for the poor. Small farms were swallowed by big landowners with either consent of or indifference from the emperor. Taxes were diligently collected from the poor, while the aristocrats enjoyed unjust tax exemptions. The emperors led meaningless wars, their armies destroying everything on the way – just like the barbarian armies had before. The people loathed the distant emperors from Constantinople and did not see them as their true leaders. Uprisings became common. By the end of the sixth century, the empire was on the edge of collapse. A mentally ill usurper called Phocas took the throne. Armies were disorganized. Goods were stolen. Slavene tribes invaded the Balkans. Mess and poverty were everywhere. But there was one part of the empire that was still thriving: North Africa. The Senate in Constantinople saw that as a chance and secretly wrote to the North African emperor, asking him to take control over the Byzantine army and save the empire from misery.

The governor of Carthage was an elderly man and was not interested in great actions, but his son, Heraclius, was. He took a fleet and went to Constantinople. He had no trouble dealing with Phocas; the mob had already lynched him as soon as they noticed the new emperor approaching in 610. But the empire had other, more serious problems: the Persians had invaded Armenia and Mesopotamia, much of the central Byzantine territory, and parts of Egypt. Even the plague had returned. It could hardly be worse. Then refugees from the east brought news that the Persians had seized Jerusalem and killed all its men. In 619, the Persians sacked Egypt. There was no free bread for the people of Byzantium anymore. The empire had no money to pay the soldiers, and Heraclius turned to the church. The patriarch Sergius gave him the entire treasures from the church, including gold and silver plates.

The War against the Persians

Heraclius did not rush to fight the Persians. Hidden behind the walls of Constantinople, he systematically reorganized the army. It took him ten years, but the result was remarkable. The army that left the safety of the city in 622 was confident and inspired by great leadership. They launched a surprise attack from the sea and crushed the Persians with unbelievable ease. Then the Byzantines went to the Persians' sacred place in present-day Azerbaijan and burned the temple of Zoroaster, avenging Jerusalem. But the position of this brave army was dangerous. They were outnumbered and could easily be surrounded from all sides, and there was no one left to protect Constantinople.

Heraclius made the decision to split the army into three parts - one was to defend the capital, and the second two were to invade different parts of the Persian Empire. The fraction led by Heraclius' brother, Theodore, won a great victory; Heraclius won another, entered Ctesiphon, and returned the True Cross, which the Persians had stolen from Jerusalem. The years when Persia caused terror were over once and for all. The Byzantine Empire finally had a glorious emperor it deserved.

Cultural Changes

By the time of Heraclius, very few people knew Latin. Greek was now the official language of the empire. Even the emperors - who used to be hailed as Imperator Caesar and Augustus - now held the title Basileus.

In 630, Heraclius went to Jerusalem to return the True Cross to where it belonged. He was yet to discover that the church was not unique, and that it was a true weakness that any future invader would exploit.

The Muslim Attack

In 622, when Heraclius was fighting Persians on the Arabian Peninsula, a man named Muhammad went from Mecca to Medina and began slaughtering the local tribes. He divided the world into two parts – *Dar al-Islam* (the House of Islam) and *Dar al-Harb* (the House of War). His followers believed their duty was to expand the House of Islam through holy jihad. In five years, the Muslim armies were ready to start their mission. The surrounding empires were weaker than ever. The Persians asked the Byzantines and the Chinese for help, but the help never came. After Persia, the Muslim army entered the Byzantine province of Syria, destroyed Damascus and, soon after, Jerusalem. By that time, Heraclius was seriously ill and unable to defend the territories. The only thing that he could do in Jerusalem was to take the True Cross with him to Constantinople. For the rest of his life, Heraclius had the feeling that God had abandoned him..

Much of the Middle East went through a deep change. Arabic replaced Greek, and Islam replaced Christianity. Eventually, Damascus and Baghdad, rather than Rome and Constantinople, had become the center of the world for them. As for the Byzantine Empire, there was no one capable of replacing Heraclius on the throne. The next five rulers were underage and without any real influence. Then the period known as the Twenty Years' Anarchy came. Numerous usurpers fought each other, pushing the empire into further chaos. Most of the East had fallen under the Islamic sword, including the whole of Egypt. Even Constantinople was in jeopardy, but eventually a new competent ruler emerged and consolidated the Byzantine force.

Chapter 6 – The Iconoclasts: Leo III the Isaurian and Constantine V

By the end of the seventh century, the Muslim forces held three of the five great Christian cities – Jerusalem, Alexandria, Antioch, and virtually every important capital in the East.[120] Constantinople wasn't unconquerable anymore – the Muslims had built a navy powerful enough to defeat the Byzantine's. Terrified, the emperor and the entire government moved from Constantinople to Sicily. The only thing that prevented the Arabs from completely destroying Constantinople was a civil war among their lines – one that still hasn't ended, between the Shiites and the Sunnites.

The next target of the forces of Islam was Afghanistan. The Byzantine administration returned to Constantinople, but the Muslims continued to overwhelm their forces. Syracuse in Sicily was destroyed, and the Arabs soon conquered North Africa. Determined to terminate Constantinople, the Arab caliphate launched yearly attacks on the city, which was now exposed from the sea. The Islamic army invaded the island of Rhodes, located across from Constantinople. Only a miracle could save the Christians. But then, a Syrian refugee from Heliopolis, called Callinicus, invented "Greek fire," an extremely flammable liquid (the exact formula was kept as a state secret and it was never revealed), which was released at the enemy fleet from great distances. Balls of textile were soaked and launched at the ships, which burnt one after another, and the sea water only made it worse for them. Constantinople was saved.

Unfortunately, the rest of the empire was utterly unprotected, and it quickly fell. In the early eighth century, the Islamic forces took Spain. Soon they felt strong enough to try again and finally invade Constantinople.

Meanwhile, a man from Syria called Konon saw his opportunity and, in the midst of chaos, seized the throne and changed his name to Leo III. Thanks to his experience fighting Arabs and the coldest winter in many years, the Muslim army was overcome and forced to return to Damascus.

The Byzantine Iconoclasm

The Byzantine Empire had endured terrible losses. Two-thirds of the territory and half the population were gone. The once-dominant empire was constrained to Asia Minor, which was now poorer and weaker than ever. The Muslims insisted that Christ was just an ordinary prophet and, for a moment, it looked like God was on their side. Was there something that the Muslims were doing right and the Christians wrong? Why had Christ withdrawn his protective hand? Was there something that had angered God? Everyone pondered over those questions, and the emperor managed to identify a single thing that could cause such destruction.

There was actually a divine commandment that the Muslims thoroughly followed and the Christians did not. The worship of icons more and more resembled the old pagan veneration of idols. As soon as he got the idea, Leo III was sure that the empire was being chastised for the sin of idolatry and determined to do whatever it took to make both the sin and the punishment stop immediately. In 725, in the Hagia Sophia, he gave a sermon that changed history. The Muslims, he stated, conquered wastelands thanks to their strict prohibition of all images. The Byzantines, on the other hand, were guilty of heresy. Then he ordered the magnificent golden icon of Christ that was placed on the main gate to the Great Palace, just above the mosaics celebrating the victories of Justinian and Belisarius, to be destroyed. It was just the beginning.

The taking down the icon of Christ provoked public outrage, and a group of women lynched the officer in charge. Occasional riots couldn't stop the emperor, who enjoyed great authority in the army, thanks to his numerous victories. But the pope in the West, as well Western Europe in its entirety, was annoyed by such actions of the Eastern emperor. Unwilling to give up their artistic heritage and pretty much unaware of the deep reasons behind all this (medieval Western Europe was protected behind the Byzantine shield and blissfully unaware of the danger from Arab expansion), the pope condemned the actions of the emperor who interfered with the church's teachings. Leo ordered the arrest of the pope, and the pope excommunicated everyone who dared to destroy an icon. This led to the most profound alienation between Christians in history to that point.[121]

In the East, innumerable images were confiscated and destroyed, and the mosaics that decorated church walls were covered with solid colors. Many images found their way to the West. Monks were leaving the monasteries, taking their icons with them. The emperor, however, was unstoppable. Leo III was winning one battle after another, and in 740 he completely expelled the Muslim forces, proving that his iconoclasm (the destruction of icons) had helped the Byzantines. One nightmare was over, and the next year the victorious emperor died peacefully in his bed.

Constantine V

The situation was far from resolved when Leo's son came to the throne. Many hoped that he would stop the appalling practice of smashing the precious artifacts. However, this emperor was raised with an intolerance for idolatry, and he soon became the most aggressive iconoclast who punished and humiliated the monks and even patriarchs who tried to resist him, confiscated the property of the most powerful monasteries, expelled monks and nuns, and lodged his troops in their lodges.

Constantine V had an impressive theological education and was able to defend his beliefs, but he still needed a legitimization from the official church. So he summoned a great council, let only his supporters express their views, and enforced a clear endorsement of iconoclasm. Icons, relics, and even prayers to the saints were all proclaimed idolatry and forbidden.

Just like his father, Constantine V was an extraordinary military commander and won some significant battles over the Bulgars and the Muslims, and his authority was indisputable. But the iconoclasm was tearing the empire apart and, at the same time, creating a distance between Asia Minor and the larger Christian communities worldwide. Because of his zeal, Constantine V had missed the historical chance to unite Christendom under his rule.

Chapter 7 – The Coldblooded Empress Irene of Athens

By the end of his rule, Constantine's military achievements had been forgotten and he was widely loathed by the populace. The iconoclastic emperor became known as *Copronymos*. He was succeeded by his son, Leo, a moderate iconoclast who tried to lower the tension that his father had created. However, he died too soon, possibly due to the intervention of his wife, Irene. Their son, Constantine VI, was only ten and way too young for the throne. So the empress de facto ruled the empire.

Irene was just an orphan from Athens until she won an empire-wide beauty contest, which Constantine V organized in order to choose a wife for his son.[122] Irene was a disastrous choice, and she was to soon become one of the most callous rulers in Byzantine history.

As a devoted opponent of iconoclasm, she carefully got rid of iconoclasts who held important positions, including her husband the emperor and the empire's best soldiers and officers. The imperial army was so weak and unmotivated that, when the Muslims came to invade parts of the empire, the soldiers simply joined them. Irene ended up having to pay for peace.

The End of Iconoclasm

The empress' main goal was to restore icons to veneration. She gathered the patriarchs of Rome, Jerusalem, Antioch, and Alexandria to the Church of the Holy Wisdom in Nicaea. The patriarchs unanimously condemned iconoclasm, but admonished the believers to turn away from worship.

But there was one thing that Irene cared for more than for the theological goals: power. She should have ended the regency period once her son turned sixteen. Constantine was already in his twenties, and she still had not let relinquished her duties. Her son was weak and easy to manipulate, but she did not use the possibility to rule from the shadow. She had to have the main role. So, she issued new coins with her images only. Then she issued a decree announcing that, as the senior emperor (not empress), she would always be superior to Constantine VI. When some generals objected, she executed them and had her son thrown into prison.

Mother and Son

As a result of the empress' outrageous actions, the military was both extremely weak and disloyal to her. The Byzantine Empire had suffered terrible losses against the Bulgars, the Arabs, and the Franks. Then soldiers revolted and masses flooded the streets of Constantinople, demanding Irene to step down. Constantine VI was released from his jail cell and raised to the throne, while his mother was put under house arrest.

Ironically, Constantine was incompetent, unambitious, and certainly not the kind of ruler the people had hoped for. Soon he deserved the tag of a coward and restored his mother to the throne. When a plot against both of them was discovered, Constantine proved himself equally ruthless. Then in 797, when the emperor's baby son died, Irene used the opportunity to give the final blow. Constantine was blinded and killed. But her decline had also begun. Even though she was the sole ruler, her army was useless, and the treasury was empty.

Meanwhile in Rome

Pope Leo III had humble origins, and by the end of the eighth century, the hostility between himself and Roman aristocracy became so intense that, one day, a gang ambushed the pope with the intention to blind him and rip out his tongue. The pontiff miraculously escaped to the king of the Franks. His enemies then charged him with several accusations, but the only one who had the authority to preside over such a trial was the emperor of the Roman Empire. At that moment, the emperor in charge in Constantinople was Irene.

The fact that the emperor was a woman bothered the pope more than her immoral past. He needed a different kind of emperor, and he came up with a cunning plan to take power from the East and give it to his allies, the Franks. Charles the Great, also known as Charlemagne, seemed perfect. Already a glorious figure, he appeared in Rome to testify on the Pope's behalf. Then, during a Christmas Mass, Leo declared Charlemagne the Holy Roman Emperor.

Pope Leo acted as if he had the authority to give and take the true crown of the Roman Empire. It was a bold move, and he needed some kind of proof. So, he made the most infamous forgery of the Middle Ages. He made a document called the "Donation of Constantine," which stated that Emperor Constantine had given Pope Sylvester (who, according to the document, had miraculously cured Constantine of leprosy) the authority over the Western Empire. It took six hundred years for the forgery to be revealed, but at that moment in history, it appeared completely authentic.

The people of Constantinople were shocked by the news that an illiterate barbarian was given the title of Roman Emperor. The next step from the west was the offer for Irene to marry Charlemagne, and she almost accepted. But this was too much for the Eastern elite. They captured and banished the empress and proclaimed the minister of finance as emperor. Irene died next year in exile in Lesbos.

Chapter 8 – Tiny Steps Forward: Theophilus and Michael the Drunkard

The empire had changed a lot by the beginning of the ninth century. The Bulgars, empowered by a great warlord called Krum, killed one Byzantine emperor, overthrew another, and caused great damage to the Byzantine army, populace, and land. New emperors turned to iconoclasm again and started burning works of art, but it didn't help. They lacked the powerful armies of Constantine V and his father had.

The situation improved rather slowly. In the ninth century, the empire was reduced to Asia Minor, Greece, and Thrace, but the situation there was stable. Regardless of who was the current emperor, the government was smaller and more efficient. New gold mines were found, resulting in a full treasury.

The Cultural Renaissance under Theophilus

The greatest improvements emerged in the sphere of education. The public interest in literacy was spreading and numerous private schools were open. In the mid-ninth century, Theophilus opened public scriptoria and started paying teachers throughout the empire. The University of Constantinople received two new faculties. Once again, the city was the cultural capital of

Europe.

Unlike any other emperor in the medieval times, Theophilus was surprisingly approachable. On one occasion, he even participated in the chariot races and amazed the spectators with his skill.

This emperor also had a habit of walking the streets of Constantinople in disguise, and once a week he went to different cities and talked to people, encouraging anyone to seek him out and sharing justice.

Finally, Theophilus started the most ambitious projects since the age of Justinian, renovated public buildings, built new ones, and gave the capital a new, lavish appearance.

New Christians

The Slavene people that settled in the Balkans weren't particularly aggressive and could be won over culturally. The pope realized this first and sent missionaries to convert them. The patriarch Photius then sent two of his men – the monks Cyril and Methodius. Even though the western missionaries came first, they insisted that Latin was the only language to be used in services. The Slavs didn't like the idea, and no further progress was made in that direction. The Byzantine monks took a different path and learned Slavic. The language had no written alphabet, so they provided one. Bulgaria and other Balkan states soon entered the Byzantine cultural orbit to which they still belong. The bonds among the states on the east were fortified in Constantinople, but the hostility between the two Christian seas – the old and new Rome – only grew bigger.

Military Recovery under Michael the Drunkard (and his Uncle)

The ninth-century Byzantine Emperors were mostly militarily incompetent. Michael the Drunkard was not an exception, and his nickname was well earned. However, under his rule, a visionary general (who happened to be Michael's uncle) called Bardas won some important battles against Muslim armies, invaded Egypt, and devastated the armies of the emirs of Mesopotamia and Armenia when they attempted to invade the Byzantine territory.

Bardas was effectively governing the empire until Michael decided to give another man, a former peasant called Basil the Macedonian (who was, in fact, Armenian and had no connections with Macedonia whatsoever) too much power. Bardas knew what was coming, but he could not convince his foolish nephew to be more careful. Basil killed Bardas personally, became Michael's co-emperor, and then had the Drunkard killed too.

Chapter 9 – A New Golden Age: Basil the Macedonian and his Dynasty

Basil's past certainly hadn't been spotless, and the future members of his dynasty (which lasted for nearly two hundred years) were uncomfortable with the way he seized the throne. Moreover, by eastern standards, he was embarrassingly uneducated,[123] but it didn't prevent him from ruling effectively. He was aware of the possibility to recover the empire, which was now smaller and easier to defend.

The emperor invested considerable amounts in rebuilding the Byzantine fleet, aware that the Muslims were not as powerful as they were only a century ago. The navy, led by Admiral Nicetas Oöryphas, quickly demonstrated its worth. In a brief action, the Byzantines got rid of the pirates raiding in the Gulf of Corinth. The time had come for a great offensive. The navy attacked Muslim territories, and by 876, vast territories, including Cyprus, northern Mesopotamia, Dalmatia, and Lombardy.

The next step in returning the glory of the empire involved the construction projects. Basil renovated old churches, adorned them with sumptuous mosaics, and overhauled public monuments. Then he built a church as impressive as Hagia Sophia. Iconoclasm had ended long ago, and the new church was rich with decoration. Basil was so engrossed in completing this church that he sacrificed Syracuse to finish it. He needed the navy to transport marble, and he simply refused to send it to Sicily.

A new cultural renaissance started thanks mostly to the patriarch Photius, who made classical Greek and Roman literature popular after so many years. Intellectual awakening spread throughout Byzantium, and the emperor initiated the translation of Justinian's law codex, originally written in Latin, into Greek. The project was not finalized during Basil's reign due to the unexpected setback. The emperor's eldest and favorite son, Constantine, unexpectedly died and left the father depressed for the rest of his life.

The Drunkard's Son, Leo VI the Wise

The next in line for the throne was his second son, Leo VI, who most probably wasn't Basil's son at all. Basil had married a mistress of Michael the Drunkard, and she was already pregnant with this son, who was now 15. The next couple of years were characterized by the antagonism between the (official) father and son. Leo had been beaten and put into prison, then released with the help of the father of his girlfriend, Zöe. It looks like Zöe's father helped his future son in law get rid of his "father" and take the throne. Basil lost the throne in nearly the same way he had helped himself to it: with lots of spilled blood.

Leo's first action as emperor was to exhume Michael the Drunkard and rebury him in the Church of the Holy Apostles. Now that he had avenged his true father and solved his private matter, he focused on politics. Intelligent and superbly educated, Leo VI was completely prepared for the role of the Byzantine emperor. Literature and architecture flourished, and the translation of Roman law was completed. The period of peace and prosperity that enabled these activities didn't just happen; it was all thanks to Leo. He brilliantly came to an idea to appoint his youngest brother, Stephen, as patriarch. Now the emperor controlled both the state and the church, and the two worked in perfect unison.

Leo the Wise, as everyone started to call him, was a great emperor, except for the fact that he wasn't much of a fighter. He actually never led his army in a battle, and his foreign policy was not as impressive as his domestic endeavors. A new hostility between the Byzantines and the Bulgars emerged when the new khan tried to restore paganism. Luckily, the Khan's own father, who had previously retired to a monastery, disposed of him and put his younger brother, Simeon, on the throne. Simeon was a Christian who spent his youth in Constantinople, but the hostility didn't stop until some non-tactical actions were taken by the emperor. Leo then employed the Magyars from the east to teach the Bulgars a lesson. Simeon, in turn, called for the Pechenegs and got rid of the Magyars. The situation was more stable on other fronts, thanks to the impressive fleet and able generals in the east. But something else was going on in the capital, and it was more interesting (if not more important) than all the battles that were led at the time.

The Love Life of an Emperor: Leo and two Zoes

Basil had not allowed Leo to marry his beloved mistress, Zoe, and he forced him to marry another woman, who was now his empress but only for a short time. The couple had no children, and she died shortly after. The emperor was finally free to marry the love of his life and have children with her, but the first child happened to be a girl, and there was no possibility that Zoe would ever give birth to another because she died in fever soon after the girl was born.

Leo was determined to produce an heir and wanted to marry again, but third marriages were forbidden by the Eastern Church. It took a great deal of patience, diplomacy, and blackmails to persuade the new patriarch to let him marry again, this time to Eudocia. His new empress gave birth to a boy and immediately died. The baby, sadly, also died just a few days later. And there seemed to be no way for Leo to ensure a blessing for a fourth marriage. The patriarch informed him that a fourth marriage would be worse than an extramarital affair, which Leo interpreted quite literally and found himself a beautiful lover, named Zoe Carbonopsina ("of the coal-black eyes"). Ironically, the couple had a son shortly after, whom they named Constantine VII.

The patriarch refused to baptize and legitimize the boy and this marriage, and requested Leo to give up Zoe, which he wasn't willing to do. The emperor then turned to the Western pope, who gave him support. Leo arrested the patriarch Nicholas for treason and replaced him with another one. Finally, he made his son his legitimate heir of the Byzantine empire and, a couple of years later, he died.

All the Regent Rulers of Young Emperor Constantine VII

The six year old Constantine was left with a hostile regent, his wicked uncle Alexander III, who immediately expelled Zoe from the palace. Furthermore, the boy was seriously ill and it was a miracle that he even survived. Alexander allegedly intended to have him castrated to prevent him from ever taking power, but thanks to his dynamic lifestyle, the malicious regent soon died of exhaustion.

The next regent was the patriarch Nicholas, whom Alexander had previously restored to power. He untactfully promised the Bulgarian ruler Simeon that the young emperor would marry his daughter, and ended up almost lynched when the people heard about his scandalous plan.

Previously exiled, Zoe Carbonopsina returned to the palace and started acting as regent for her son. Refusing to keep the promise that the patriarch Nicholas had given to the Bulgars, she entered the war. An issue broke out when a Byzantine admiral named Romanus Lecapenus refused to transport the Pechenegs, whom Zoe hired to invade Bulgaria, and left the Byzantine army at the mercy of the Bulgars, who of course took the opportunity and decimated the abandoned soldiers. Zoe's credibility was irreparably ruined, and she decided to marry Leo Phocas, a patrician and successful commander who won some great battles at the Black Sea coast.

Constantine VII was thirteen at the time, and there was a danger that the empress' new husband would eliminate him, so his supporters reached out to the spotless Admiral Romanus Lecapenus. He agreed to protect the young emperor, became the head of the imperial guard, and had the young Constantine marry his daughter. Subsequently, he took all power and became the senior emperor. However, Romanus I Lecapenus wasn't cruel by nature and would never physically hurt Constantine, but he promoted his sons Christopher, Stephen, and Constantine as his co-emperors and gave them an advantage over Constantine VII. Romanus I victoriously ended the war with Bulgaria and was responsible for the great conquests of John Curcuas in the east.

Suddenly, Romanus' eldest son, Christopher – who was meant for the throne – died. His younger brothers, Stephen and Constantine, were spoiled, corrupt, and cruel, and Romanus started feeling guilty for usurping the throne. In his late age, he revoked his earlier decisions and made Constantine VII his exclusive heir. The outraged sons had their father captured and sent off to a distant monastery. But the people of Constantinople did not want any of them on the throne. The time had finally come for Constantine VII to rule in his own right.

Constantine VII "the Purple-born"

While Constantine was heavily ignored in the palace, the Byzantine populace loved him and felt the injustice made against him. He was, after all, a "purple-born," a true son of Macedon, and the Lecapeni were merely usurpers. When the news broke that Constantine's life was in danger, the angry crowd forced the widely despised Lecapeni brothers to acknowledge him as the senior emperor.

Constantine VII[124]
https://commons.wikimedia.org/wiki/File:Constantine_VII_Porphyrogenitus.jpg

Constantine was already thirty-nine, and was more decisive than anyone expected. He sent the Lecapeni brothers into exile and then continued the policy that Romanus led remarkably well. The only difference was that he replaced some men at the top of the army, favoring the Phocas family, which was at odds with the Lecapeni. A fantastic general, Nicephorus Phocas, together with his nephew, John Tzimisces, emerged victorious against the emir of Syria, conquered cities on the river Euphrates and came near Antioch. Nicephorus soon became known as the "Pale Death of the Saracens," and Muslim forces would abandon the field when they got word that he was on the way.

The Byzantine empire was powerful again. Even though the army was busy on the Syrian border, it still had the capacity to crush the Magyars, who optimistically tried to invade Thrace. But the cultural power of Constantinople grew even bigger. The members of European royal elites were often the guests of Constantine VII, who never ceased to impress them. The eloquent and charismatic emperor left such a powerful impression on the Russian regent princess, Olga, that she promptly decided to convert herself – and subsequently her people – to Christianity.

Constantine died of fever, and the power passed to his son, Romanus II.

Romanus II and Theophano

Unlike his father, Romanus II was born and raised entitled. He never lacked anything and his father abided all his wishes. The problem was that young Romanus wanted to marry Theophano – a woman of modest origin and, as we'll see, not so modest ambition. The marriage was utterly inappropriate, but Constantine did not want to spoil his son's happiness, and the couple happily married and bore a son, whom they named Basil II.

Romanus II found administration rather boring and spent his days hunting. Although he was under the huge influence of his wife, the people who effectively led the empire were two men. One of them was the chamberlain Joseph Bringas, a eunuch who managed to further improve the University of Constantinople, the arts, and the economy of the empire. The second man was Nicephorus Phocas, who continued to win battle after battle and expelled the Arab pirates from Crete. His brother, Leo Phocas, and nephew, John Tzimisces, conquered Syria and Mesopotamia, crushing fifty-five fortresses on the way, and entered Aleppo.[125] When they returned, they heard that Romanus II (twenty-two at the time) was dead. According to rumors, he was poisoned by his wife, Theophano. The truth was that he got badly injured while hunting, but this remained a secret because hunting was forbidden during the fast of Lent. The situation was tense, and it was going to be worse.

Chapter 10 – The Change in the House of Macedon: Nicephorus Phocas and His Nephew

No matter how ambitious the empress Teophano was, and no matter how little affection she felt for her husband, she probably never really thought of killing him. Now that he was gone, her position was desperate. Her son, Basil, was still a small child, which made both of them extremely vulnerable. A strong figure was needed to protect the underage emperor, and her mother called for Nicephorus Phocas, the most brilliant Byzantine war commander since Belisarius. The greatest opponent of this idea was the chamberlain Joseph Bringas, who promptly used the influence he still had and released a decree banning the general from the city. However, the closed gates of the city couldn't prevent Nicephorus from entering. He was wildly popular, and crowds soon required that Nicephorus be allowed to enter Constantinople.

When other schemes failed, Joseph wrote to John Tzimisces, the nephew of Nicephorus, and offered him the imperial crown. Tzimisces, however, showed the letter to his uncle, who was proclaimed emperor by his soldiers the following day. The chamberlain continued with desperate measures, jailed all the members of the Phocas family, and eliminated all boats, ferries, and other vessels that could transport anyone into Constantinople. But it was a matter of time when the crowds would erupt, and it soon happened. The Chamberlain lost control over the city,

Nicephorus entered, and the patriarchs instantly crowned him.

The Emperor Nicephorus and Theophano

A natural-born leader with vast military experience and numerous victories, Nicephorus was more than qualified to rule Byzantium. But he was so much different from the cultivated men that until very recently sat on the imperial throne. Nicephorus was rude, used to giving orders, short-tempered, and prone to insulting anyone who annoyed him.

The empress-dowager Theophano welcomed him warmly as the protector of her child. He was over fifty, and she was twenty-two. He was an handsome soldier, and she was lovely. Within a month, he proposed her to marry him, which she gladly accepted. But life kept moving on, and soon he was on a campaign again.

Imperial Expansion under Nicephorus

Nicephorus' nephew, John Tzimisces, was already in Syria when the emperor joined him. Together they conquered Aleppo and Cilicia and reduced what used to be a mighty emirate into a vassal state.

The emperor was so good at fighting the Muslims in the east, but his tactlessness proved disastrous in the west. On one occasion, the representatives of the German Emperor Otto I made a mistake and addressed Nicephorus as king of the Greeks. He got so mad that he threw them into a dungeon, which almost resulted in a war against the two empires. The even worse incident occurred when a Bulgarian ambassador came requesting their regular small tribute (which was, in fact, a fixed amount used to cover the cost of a Byzantine princess at the Bulgarian court, which enabled her to live in a way appropriate for her status). Nicephorus became furious and disbelievingly asked if they thought he was a slave. Then he told them he would come in person to pay the tribute they deserved.

Nicephorus paid the Russians to attack Bulgaria for him, and they did so easily. But then the Russians, led by Prince Svyatoslav, simply replaced the Bulgarians, and they were much more aggressive than the former neighbors of Byzantium.

In the next couple of years, he would return to the eastern frontiers to reconquer Armenia and Antioch, but he had some unsolved domestic issues that prevented him from proceeding and retaking Jerusalem.

The Holy Mountain

Nicephorus believed that soldiers who died resisting the forces of Islam should be respected as martyrs. The patriarch firmly refused such a possibility and rejected the notion of "holy warriors" (in the west, as we'll see, such an idea was accepted and that's exactly how the Crusades had begun).

However, this wasn't the only thing that annoyed the emperor. He was constantly marching through Byzantine lands and was fully aware of the prevailing materialism. The church possessed boundless land. Monastic houses were lavish, filled with gold and invaluable frescoes, and bounded by fruitful vineyards. At the same time, the church did not pay any taxes. All this seemed unfair to the emperor Nicephorus Phocas, who decided to put an end to it by issuing several decrees which forbade donating land to the corrupt church.

The emperor thought that monks should live in simple monasteries away from the urban noise. To demonstrate his idea, Nicephoros sent his close friend, the monk Athanasius, to Greece to establish a monastery on the hills of Mount Athos. Then he made the new monastic community (which still exists today and wears the Byzantine flag) autonomous of the patriarch, responsible directly to the throne.

Decline and Death

Despite all his triumphs, the emperor became unpopular in Constantinople. The church was no longer his ally, and everyone else was enraged by ever-increasing taxes. Moreover, there was a rumor that his brother was trying to kill the young princes, Basil and Constantine, yet Nicephorus took no actions against Leo.

A prophecy announced that Nicephorus would be killed in his palace by the hand of one of his own citizens, so he erected a massive wall separating the Great Palace from the rest of the city. The people loathed him, and he used every opportunity to leave Constantinople and find his peace on the real battlefield.

Meanwhile, Theophano had fallen in love with John Tzimisces, the emperor's nephew. The young general was not in favor of the emperor, and the two lovers arranged the murder. Nicephorus was brutally humiliated and butchered during the night by the assassins hidden in the empress' half of the palace. The next day, John Tzimisces was hailed as the Roman Emperor. Theophano was not that lucky. The patriarch ordered Tzimisces to get rid of her if he wanted to be crowned, and he did not object to him.

The Emperor John I Tzimisces

John Tzimisces was both a glorious war commander and a pleasant, well-educated man, the ideal of a true statesman. His first action as the emperor was to get rid of any resistance in Constantinople and once that had been settled, he went to the Balkans. The situation there was quite a mess, thanks to Nicephorus' diplomatic failures. The Russians were openly stating that they would invade Byzantine territory. So, the new emperor led forty thousand troops, smashed the Russians' defenses, and liberated the king of the Bulgars. One more battle and it was all over. The prince of Kiev left Bulgaria with only handful of men; everyone else was dead.

John annexed Bulgaria and moved on. The Fatimids of Egypt were threatening the Byzantine territory in Syria. They already defeated one smaller imperial army and invaded Antioch, and now the time had come for the empire to strike back, and it was one of the most notable military campaigns in the history of the Byzantine Empire. John I Tzimisces started from the north, conquered Mosul, pursued the Muslims down the coast of the Mediterranean and took all the cities of Syria and Palestine on the way: Baalbek, Beirut, Damascus, Tiberias, Acre, Caesarea, Tripoli. He entered Nazareth, the hometown of Jesus Christ, but just like Nicephorus, he postponed the liberation of Jerusalem.

The Byzantine empire was now more powerful than it had been in centuries. All the enemies were devastated, and the emperor was pleased. But when he tried to investigate the origin of the vast properties in the possession of aristocrats, his chamberlain, Basil Lecapenus, poisoned him. Within a couple of days, the great conqueror was dead.

Chapter 11 – Basil II the Bulgar Slayer

The son of Romanus II and Theophano, Basil II, had been growing up while Nicephorus Phocas and John Tzimisces were in charge of the empire. Now that both of them were dead and he was an adult, he could legitimately take the throne, but there were a few obstacles. The first was the head chamberlain, Basil Lecapenus, who was too powerful and equally unwilling to hand over power. The second problem was the notion that in the lengthy history of the Macedon Dynasty, the most competent rulers were the generals and not those who had grown up in the palace.

A general called Bardas Sclerus claimed he was a better choice for the throne, began a revolt, and was promptly hailed as emperor by the masses. Panicked, Basil Lecapenus sent for the exiled general Bardas Phocas, who also wanted to seize the throne, but was the only one who could fight Sclerus. The two armies fought for three years, Phocas won, and returned to fight the Saracens.

The Rise of the Legitimate Emperor

Near the end of the tenth century, Basil Lecapenus was pleased by the way he managed to get rid of both powerful generals. His position was perfect - he held all the power, keeping the incompetent and unambitious emperor as a mask for his deeds - except that the emperor was neither incompetent nor unambitious. Basil II hit the chamberlain out of the blue and had him arrested for conspiring against the emperor. Lecapenus' lands and his wealth were finally confiscated. Basil II was twenty-five and was fully ready to rule the empire.

However, the first military expedition of the new emperor turned out to be disastrous. He went to fight the Bulgars, who meanwhile consolidated under Tsar Samuel. The Byzantine army was caught in an ambush. The emperor fled the field, but most of his army, as well as his reputation, were destroyed.

Then, both Bardas Sclerus and Bardas Phocas decided to try and seize the throne. They even united against the emperor, but Phocas almost immediately arranged for Sclerus to be arrested, and he continued alone.

Alliance with the Russians

The emperor in Constantinople knew he had a problem. The Bulgars were aggressively invading the Balkan peninsula, and he desperately needed an army, but not one led by Phocas. So he reached out to the Russian Prince Vladimir, gave him his sister as a wife, and received a powerful ally and the Varangian Guard – an army of huge, terrifying soldiers who helped him deal with Bardas Phocas first, and then with the Fatimid army in Tripoli, and finally the Bulgars.

Safe with his Varangian Guard, Basil II decided to deal with the nobility, forcing the aristocrats to return the land they had taken during the last few decades. In addition to that, he issued a decree instructing that if a farmer couldn't pay his taxes, his wealthy neighbor was obliged to pay for him.

The Bulgar Slayer

Basil, the Bulgar Slayer, earned his nickname when, after the final battle against Tsar Samuel, he ordered all the prisoners to be blinded, leaving one eye here and there, so that they should find their way home. Now, for the first time since the Slavic tribes came, the entire Balkan Peninsula was under Byzantine control. The empire doubled in size during his reign, and it grew stronger. Basil II knew how important it was to govern new territories properly. Good governance certainly lessened the tension, but Basil used some new means to reach his goals.

In 1012, the Fatimid caliph ordered the destruction of all churches in his territory. Basil II didn't rush into a battle. He reacted with an economical measure and forbade all trade with the Fatimids. When he had to fight, he gladly did, and he always won. The empire now spread from the Danube to the Euphrates. Basil's sixty-four-year reign was the most successful one in Byzantine history. He died of old age while planning a campaign. Unfortunately, he did not have an heir – the fact that always pushed empires into crisis.

Chapter 12 – Alexius Comnenus

The period that came after the death of Basil II was one of constant decline. Mediocrities came to the throne one after another, the economy weakened, and the army completely relied on mercenaries. Then in 1054, the Christian Church split in half. The Latin Catholic ("universal") Church was maintained by the pope, and the Greek Orthodox ("true") was managed by the patriarch. The divide was profound, and the consequences were yet to be felt.

Another setback emerged in the eleventh century when the aggressive Seljuk Turks began invading the imperial territory. A single event that best illustrates the poor health of the empire took place in 1071. The Byzantine army, led by the emperor Romanus Diogenes, managed to push the Seljuks back across the Euphrates. The aristocrats weren't happy about it. A strong emperor could easily limit their privileges, and they did not want to let that happen. So they betrayed him in the decisive moment, sacrificing the best Byzantine soldiers along with the emperor. It was the most obvious sign of almost unreparable decline.

The fight for power between the ambitious aristocrats lasted for ten years, during which many emerged and fell, causing the prolongation of the civil war. New hope emerged in 1081 when the general Alexius Comnenus was crowned.

A Faulty Start

The Comnenus family had always been at odds with the Macedonian dynasty, and Alexius – who seized the throne by killing his predecessor – seemed like yet another usurper. Immediately after his victory, the mercenaries from the army he had employed started robbing Constantinople. It was the first bad sign. The second was the invasion of the Normans, who were now terribly close to the port in Dalmatia that offers direct access to Via Egnatia and the Byzantine capital.

Alexius' army consisted of the Varangian Guard and various mercenaries. The Varangians fought bravely and efficiently against the Normans, but the Turkish mercenaries betrayed them. The bulk of the Byzantine army was butchered.

Alternative Ways

The next time when Alexius had to encounter the Normans, he chose the way of diplomacy. The German Emperor Henry IV, thankful for the gold he had received from the Byzantine Emperor, agreed to attack the common enemy – the Norman Commander Guiscard. The Germans invaded Italy, and the pope was forced to beg the chief Norman to return immediately. Then Alexius reduced Venetian tariffs. The Norman forces depended on Venetian merchants, and now they were left without supplies.

The Norman threat was diminished, and the Muslim enemy was split and inefficient, but the Seljuk Turks were dangerous, and Alexius did not have a proper army. He needed support, and he came to an idea.

The First Crusade

In 1095, Alexius wrote to Pope Urban, informing him of Turkish conquests – most notably the one of the Holy Land – and asking him to send some support to fellow Christians against the Saracens. The pope then delivered a speech in Clermont, France, declaring that "all those who marched with a pure heart would have their sins absolved."[126] The crowd responded enthusiastically. Knights and peasants of all sorts from Italy, France, and Germany started flooding Constantinople. The Crusade seemed like a march on the Byzantine capital, and not the liberation of Jerusalem, and the people involved responded to the pope, not Alexius. One of the crusading knights was the son of Norman Robert Guiscard, from Normandy.

The first group of crusaders consisted of a monk called Peter the Hermit, and a crowd of random, undisciplined people who set fire in many towns on the way to Constantinople and, mistakenly or not, killed many of the Greek population in Asia Minor, only to get beaten by the Turks. The other groups were more serious, but they presented a much bigger threat to the attractive city of Constantinople than to the Turks. Alexius managed to make some kind of deal with them, but some strange conflicts arose on the ground of Asia Minor.

When the crusaders came to Nicaea, the city garrison selected to submit to the Byzantine commander immediately shut the gates to avoid the sack of the city, which was predominantly Christian.

The First Crusade was surprisingly successful. The Crusaders entered Jerusalem in 1099 and killed nearly everyone they found there. Then, in contrast with the given oath, the knights installed themselves as kings of seized towns, which they should have returned to the Byzantine empire.

Hostility grew, and Alexius had to face the Norman Prince Bohemond, who besieged the city and port his father had taken over twenty years ago. Just as before, Alexius cut off his supplies and, by the end of the year, made him surrender and then leave the east, never to return.

Manuel I Comnenus

The Second Crusade happened during the reign of Manuel Comnenus, the grandson of Alexius. He managed to subdue the crusader kingdoms, make the Seljuk Turks accept vassal status, and annex Serbia and Bosnia.

The Crusaders were shocked with the Byzantine's treaty with the Muslims, and the west looked at the Greeks as heretics who didn't care about the "holy war," completely missing the point that there's no such thing as a holy war in peaceful Orthodox Christianity.

The west was building animosity against the Byzantine empire, but the Eastern emperor felt secure for the moment. It looked like the empire was recovering, but it was merely an illusion that wasn't going to last. After his death, everything started to fall again.

Chapter 13 – The Collapse and Fall of the Eastern Roman Empire

There was no great leader to save Byzantium from collapse. During the reign of the underage Alexius II Comnenos, the Turks simply entered Asia Minor, and there was no one to protect it. At the same time, Serbia declared independence, and the Hungarians seized Bosnia and Dalmatia. Emperor Andronicus the Terrible was corrupt and cruel to his subjects but ineffective in foreign affairs. His successor, Isaac Angelus had no authority to rule whatsoever.

During the time of the reign of Isaac Angelus, the Kurdish sultan Saladin united the Muslim forces and Jerusalem fell again. Another crusade was launched, and Isaac proved utterly incompetent by throwing the German ambassadors in prison before apologizing to them. He made one disastrous decision after another and came to the idea to dismiss the imperial navy and let Venice take care of its sea defenses. This idea inspired his brother Alexius III to throw the emperor into a dungeon along with his son. He himself, however, was not much of a ruler either. He was only interested in helping himself to the money for his extravagant parties.[127]

Then another crusading army approached. The third crusade wasn't successful, and now it was time for the fourth, led by Frederick Barbarossa and Richard the Lionheart. Richard wanted to conquer Egypt, and he needed Venetian ships to take them over, but the Duke of Venetia refused to help without either an outrageously high reward or help to return the city of Zara, which had been taken by the Hungarians.

The Fatal Crusade

At Zara, there was a young fugitive who joined the Crusade - Alexius IV, the son of Isaac II - who had been smuggled from the prison and had been waiting for the opportunity to seize the throne ever since. He promised the crusaders enormous sums and control over the Byzantine church, if only they would help him to the throne. The warriors of the Fourth Crusade were now directed to Constantinople, and they had been told by the Duke of Venice that the Greeks were heretics.

Alexius III fled the city as soon as he realized what was happening. The crusaders released Isaac from prison and now they were waiting for the promised reward. Then they confiscated all they could find, which was only half of the sum that was discussed. They opened tombs to take reliquaries and tore the ornaments from the churches and the jewels from the coverings of ancient manuscripts. In the end, the crusaders burned numerous buildings throughout the city. The most precious churches and palaces burned. Constantinople had never been conquered before, and now it was devastated.

The Aftermath of Destruction and a Short-Lived Recovery

Pope Innocent was shocked and appalled when he heard what happened. He immediately realized what consequences it would have. He excommunicated everyone who was involved, but the damage could never be fixed. Many of the crusaders didn't care whatsoever. They had split estates among each other, crowned a Latin emperor, and put a prostitute on the patriarchal throne.[128]

Surprisingly, the people in small towns and villages were well off. The newcomers on the throne had no means whatsoever to collect the taxes, and now everything stayed in private hands. Culture and the arts flourished, sponsored by private individuals. But the days of imperial power were gone.

The heirs of Byzantine emperors started emerging throughout the Mediterranean, claiming their right to the throne. The patriarch crowned Theodore Lascaris in Nicaea. Then, the Latin Empire of Constantinople fell into the hands of the Bulgars, who did not object that Theodore Lascaris reconquer as much as he could. But another enemy emerged.

In 1242, a frightening Mongol horde came. The Mongols had already overwhelmed a Turkish army. The Seljuk sultan was forced to become his vassal. But they made no damage to Nicaea, where all important Byzantine officials were located. Through various diplomatic activities,

Nicaea undermined the Latin Empire. The Crusaders were able to control only Constantinople. They had no sustainable economy, and the only thing they were capable of doing was searching for more hidden relics.

Michael Palaeologus

In 1259, a new emperor was crowned in Nicaea, a young general named Michael Palaeologus. He immediately started diplomatic activities and sent his junior emperor, Alexius Strategopoulos, to observe how strong Constantinople's fortifications were. With the help of local farmers, Strategopoulos managed to open the gates of the city and the next day, the Byzantine forces returned to their city. The Latins panicked and fled on all sides. Since no one came to kill them, they all managed to leave safely.

Michael Palaeologus had never been to Constantinople before. Now he entered as a victor before being crowned in Hagia Sophia. Soon he started with reparation works and redesigned the flag of the empire.

The army he led was small, yet efficient, and managed to deal with all the traditional enemies, such as the Bulgars and the Turks, but a new enemy emerged. Charles of Anjou was invited by Pope Urban IV to take care of Sicily. Then the exiled Latin emperor of Constantinople, Baldwin II, offered him the Peloponnese if he would help him back to the throne. Michael VIII then wrote to the pope to help him and call Anjou back. In return, he submitted the eastern Byzantine church to the authority of the pope. The patriarch, however, refused to ratify the document. Michael Paleologus later managed to ensure the support of Spanish king and overwhelm Charles of Anjou. He was one of the better emperors Byzantium had during its final stage. The last two centuries were full of incapable emperors. During that time, a new enemy emerged, ready to give the final blow to the once powerful empire.

The Ottomans

The balance of power in the east was rapidly changing, and many Turkish tribes were coming to stay. A group of Turks called Gazi (the "swords of God"; later known as the Ottoman warriors) and their leader, Osman, aimed at capturing Constantinople. They took city after a city in the Byzantine empire and quickly came near the walls of the capital. Meanwhile, the bubonic plague spread throughout the empire. When an earthquake hit Gallipoli a couple of years later. The Turks, believing that God had given them a sign, settled in the city. Soon they surrounded Constantinople but were still unable to break in.

Anticipating a catastrophe, the Byzantine Emperor, John V, sent out appeals for help to all Christian kingdoms and empires, wrote a heartfelt letter to the pope, and even converted to

Catholicism.[129] However, he was largely ignored, and the help from the west never came. The only support came from the Balkans, where Tsar Lazar gathered a coalition of Serbian nobles and their armies and slowed down the Ottoman advance. However, in 1389, at the battle of Kosovo, Lazar, as well as most other Serbian leaders, were killed. The Ottoman sultan Murad was also killed by a Serbian knight, Milos Obilic, who acted as if he was going to desert the Serbian army the night before the battle. Milos was brought before the sultan and was quick enough to kill the Ottoman leader before his guards managed to react and hack him apart.

John V was taken aback by the news. There was no surviving force to help Constantinople, and he was ready to sacrifice whatever it took to save the city from destruction. He wrote a letter to the new sultan Bayezid, offering to become his vassal in exchange for the Byzantine capital to remain intact. Now the Turks had officially become the masters of the Eastern Christian empire.

The new Byzantine emperor, John's son, Manuel II, showed more integrity than his father, but his plans were soon broken when Bayezid "the Thunderbolt" demonstrated his power again and took the title Sultan of Rome.

Manuel wasn't willing to give up. Bayezid started a long siege against Constantinople, but during a brief period of the sultan's absence, Manuel II and his wife, the Serbian princess Helena Dragases, went to Venice, and then to many European capitals, asking for support against the Muslims. Unlike his father, Manuel was dignified and impressive, and everyone welcomed him warmly. However, it had no real effect. The western rulers were too busy fighting their own battles and they never showed up in the East for support.

An unlikely force saved Constantinople. The Mongol warlord, Timur the Lame, also known as Tamerlane, came from Uzbekistan aiming to restore the empire of his ancient predecessor, Genghis Khan. His empire was huge by the beginning of the fifteenth century, and now he came to conquer Asia Minor. Bayezid needed to defend his new territory, and so he suspended the actions against Constantinople.

Ottoman forces suffered terrible losses against Timur's army, and Bayezid ended up captured and horribly humiliated. But eventually, the Mongols headed to the Far East, determined to conquer China, leaving the Ottomans behind.

The new Ottoman sultan, Bayezid's son, Süleyman, agreed to become Manuel's vassal, but in doing so, he allowed himself time to consolidate and attack again. Manuel II returned to Constantinople as a savior in 1403, but the triumph didn't last long. Süleyman's brother, Musa, overthrew the sultan and attacked Constantinople. Manuel II then helped their third brother, Mehmed, overthrow Musa. The newest sultan was an educated, cultured man, and was ever since loyal to Manuel.

In 1422, after Mehmed had died, his son, Mustafa, sieged Constantinople. Manuel accepted the position of Turkish vassal, but he managed to prevent the Anatolian warriors from entering the city. Constantinople was safe for a brief time but remained surrounded by Turkish forces.

During the reign of Manuel's son, John VIII, Murad II invaded the city of Thessalonica, announcing that Constantinople would be next. Just like many before him, John asked the pope for help, and promised he would submit to the western church. In 1443, the new army of crusaders, this time led by the Hungarian king Ladislas and the general John Hunyadi, conquered Bulgaria. Murad II offered a ten-year truce, but the crusader army had broken it quickly. They went to the coast of the Black Sea, where the superior Ottoman forces waited and devastated them, killing King Ladislas. John Hunyadi continued to resist for a couple of years, but was overwhelmed by 1448, when John VIII was forced to congratulate Murad II on the triumph. He died shortly after that humiliating day.

The Last Emperor of Constantinople

The youngest and most able son of Manuel II, Constantine XI Dragases was crowned in 1449. During the latest Crusade, he managed to retake Athens and the surrounding areas. But now the Ottomans reconsolidated, reconquered Athens, and were in at the walls of Constantinople. A new age had begun, and the Turkish conquerors brought several cannons with them. It took five days for the walls to be breached. Afterward, the Ottomans then proceeded to the Balkans, leaving the Byzantine capital behind.

Murad II spent some time fighting Skanderg in Dalmatia, and then died. His successor, Mehmed II, a poet and scholar, claimed he was devoted to peace with Byzantium. Yet he was also a cruel ruler who had his younger brother killed just in case.

In 1453, Mehmed's men were armed with superior, newly-built cannons. When Constantine refused to surrender, they opened fire. After forty-eight days, the wall was still in place. Then the sultan changed the approach and entered into the imperial harbor with seventy ships.

The final attack took place on May 29. The remaining citizens gathered in Hagia Sophia, and the last emperor gave a final speech, reminding his populace that they were the heirs of ancient heroes. During that night, the Turks entered the city. The defenders fought till the very end and managed to resist until the Janissaries – the elite troops made of the children taken from the Christians – came and the Genovese mercenaries who helped Constantine until this very moment started retreating. Constantine had more than one opportunity to escape but refused to leave his people. He died during the terrible carnage that followed.

The people of Constantinople believed in an old legend that an angel would protect Hagia Sophia from the Turks, and many citizens gathered there. But no angel appeared, and they were all slaughtered.

Hagia Sophia was converted to a mosque. All men of noble birth were killed, and children were sold into slavery. Constantinople became the capital of the Ottoman Empire, and the sultan took the title of Caesar. The once-unparalleled empire ceased to exist.

Conclusion

After the ages of resistance, the Byzantine empire fell into the Ottoman hands, but at least it prevented the Muslim advance into Europe during the age of their aggressive expansion.[130] Now that the Turks managed to conquer the city of Constantine, they lacked the power to proceed to the now much stronger Western Europe. The Ottomans could not break the walls of Vienna, and they started retreating shortly thereafter.

Numerous refugees from Byzantium came into Western Europe and enriched the period of humanism and renaissance by bringing ancient Greek and Roman artifacts and manuscripts, including Plato's Iliad and many others. Not all exiles fled to the West. Many went to Russia, the last free Orthodox state. The peoples and nations that once belonged to the Byzantine cultural orbit are still connected by the Orthodox Church. The immense Byzantine heritage continued to live in various forms throughout the world.

The Timeline of the Byzantine Emperors

The list of all emperors and dynasties of the Byzantine Empire, including less significant ones who haven't been mentioned in this book.

CONSTANTINIAN DYNASTY (324-363)

324–353	Constantine the Great	
353–361	Constantius	*Son of Constantine the Great*
361–363	Julian the Apostate	*Cousin of Constantius*

NON-DYNASTIC

363–364	*Jovian*	Soldier, chosen on the battlefield
364–378	*Valens*	Brother of Western Emperor Valentinian

THEODOSIAN DYNASTY (379-457)

379–395	Theodosius I the Great	*Soldier, chosen by Western Emperor Gratian*
395–408	Arcadius	*Son of Theodosius*
408–450	Theodosius II	*Son of Arcadius*
450–457	Marcian	*Married Theodosius II's sister*

LEONID DYNASTY (457-518)

457–474	Leo I the Thracian	*Soldier, chosen by Eastern general Aspar*
474	Leo II	*Grandson of Leo I*
474–475	Zeno	*Son-in-law of Leo I*
475–476	Basiliscus	*Usurper, brother-in-law of Leo I*
476–491	Zeno (again)	
491–518	Anastasius I	*Son-in-law of Leo I*

JUSTINIAN DYNASTY (527-602)

518–527	Justin I	*Commander of the Palace Guard*
527–565	Justinian I the Great	*Nephew of Justin I*
565–578	Justin II	*Nephew of Justinian*
578–582	Tiberius II	*Adopted by Justin II*
582–602	Maurice	*Son-in-law of Tiberius II*

NON-DYNASTIC

602–610	Phocas	*Usurper, soldier of Maurice*

HERACLIUS DYNASTY (610-711)

610–641	Heraclius	*Usurper, general from Carthage*
641	*Constantine III*	Son of Heraclius Son of Heraclius Son of Constantine III
641	Heraclonas	
641–668	Constans II the Bearded	
668–685	Constantine IV	*Son of Constans II*
685–695	Justinian II the Slit-Nosed	*Son of Constantine IV*
695–698	*Leontius*	Usurper, soldier of Justinian II
698–705	*Tiberius III*	Usurper, Germanic naval officer of Leontius
705–711	Justinian II (again)	

NON-DYNASTIC

711–713	*Philippicus*	Usurper, Armenian soldier of Justinian II
713–715	*Anastasius II*	Usurper, imperial secretary of Philippicus
715–717	*Theodosius III*	Usurper, tax collector and son (?) of Tiberius III

ISAURIAN DYNASTY (717-802)

717–741	Leo III the Isaurian	*Usurper, Syrian diplomat of Justinian II*
741–775	Constantine V the Dung-Named	*Son of Leo III*
775–780	Leo IV the Khazar	*Son-in-law of Leo III*
780–797	Constantine VI the Blinded	*Son of Leo IV*
797–802	Irene the Athenian	*Wife of Leo IV, mother of Constantine VI*

NICEPHORUS DYNASTY (802-813)

802–811	Nicephorus I	*Usurper, finance minister of Irene*
811	*Stauracius*	Son of Nicephorus I
811–813	Michael I Rangabe	*Son-in-law of Nicephorus I*

NON-DYNASTIC

813–820	Leo V the Armenian	*Patrician and general of Michael I*

AMORIAN DYNASTY (820-867)

820–829	Michael II the Stammerer	*Son-in-law of Constantine VI*
829–842	Theophilus	*Son of Michael II*
842–855	Theodora	*Wife of Theophilus*
842–867	Michael III the Drunkard	*Son of Theophilus*

MACEDONIAN DYNASTY (867-1056)

867–886	Basil I the Macedonian	*Armenian peasant, married Michael III's widow*
886–912	Leo VI the Wise	*Son of Basil I or Michael III*
912–913	Alexander	*Son of Basil I*
913–959	Constantine VII the Purple-Born	*Son of Leo VI*
920–944	Romanus I Lecapenus	*General, father-in-law of Constantine VII*
959–963	Romanus II the Purple-Born	*Son of Constantine VII*
963–969	Nicephorus II Phocas	*General, married Romanus II's widow*
969–976	John I Tzimisces	*Usurper, nephew of Nicephorus II*
976–1025	Basil II the Bulgar-Slayer	*Son of Romanus II*
1025–1028	Constantine VIII	*Son of Romanus II*
1028–1050	*Zoë*	Daughter of Constantine VIII

1028–1034 .... Romanus III Argyrus .... *Zoë's first husband*
1034–1041 .... Michael IV the Paphlagonian .... *Zoë's second husband*
1041–1042 .... Michael V the Caulker .... *Zoë's adopted son*
1042 .... Zoë and Theodora .... *Daughters of Constantine VIII*
1042–1055 .... Constantine IX Monomachus .... *Zoë's third husband*
1055–1056 .... Theodora (again)

NON-DYNASTIC
1056–1057 .... Michael VI the Old .... *Chosen by Theodora*
1057–1059 .... Isaac I Comnenus .... *Usurper, general of Michael VI*

DUCAS DYNASTY (1059-1081)
1059–1067 .... Constantine X .... *Chosen by Isaac*
1068–1071 .... Romanus IV Diogenes .... *Married Constantine X's widow*
1071–1078 .... Michael VII the Quarter-Short .... *Son of Constantine X*
1078–1081 ...... Nicephorus III Botaneiates .... *Usurper, general of Michael VII*

COMNENIAN DYNASTY (1081-1185)
1081–1118 .... Alexius I .... *Usurper, nephew of Isaac I*
1118–1143 .... John II the Beautiful .... *Son of Alexius I*
1141–1180 .... Manuel I the Great .... *Son of John II*
1080–1183 .... Alexius II .... *Son of Manuel I*
1183–1185 .... Andronicus the Terrible .... *Usurper, cousin of Manuel I*

ANGELUS DYNASTY (1185-1204)
1185 –1195 ...... Isaac II Ángelus .... *Great-grandson of Alexius I*
1195–1203 .... Alexius III Ángelus .... *Brother of Isaac II*
1203–1204 .... Isaac II (again) and son Alexius IV

NON-DYNASTIC
1204 .... Alexius V the Bushy-Eyebrowed ..... *Usurper, son-in-law of Alexius III*

PALAEOLOGIAN DYNASTY (1259-1453)
1259–1282 .... Michael VIII .... *Great-grandson of Alexius III*
1282–1328 .... Andronicus II .... *Son of Michael VIII*
1328–1341 .... Andronicus III .... *Grandson of Andronicus II*

1341–1391 .... John V .... *Son of Andronicus III*
1347–1354 .... John VI .... *Father-in-law of John V*
1376–1379 .... Andronicus IV .... *Son of John V*
1390 .... John VII .... *Son of Andronicus IV*
1391–1425 .... Manuel II .... *Son of John V*
1425–1448 .... John VIII .... *Son of Manuel II*
1448–1453 .... Constantine XI Dragases................. *Son of Manuel II*

Here's another book by Captivating History that you might like

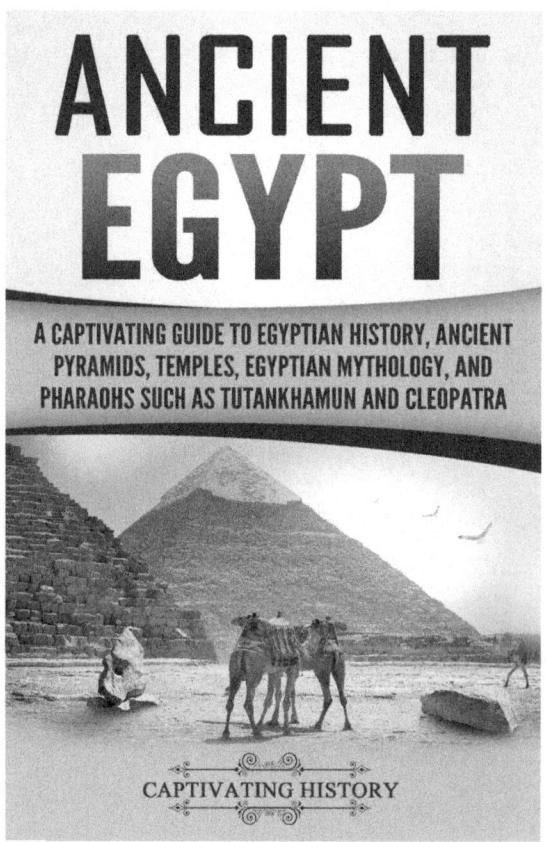

Free Bonus from Captivating History (Available for a Limited time)

Hi History Lovers!

Now you have a chance to join our exclusive history list so you can get your first history ebook for free as well as discounts and a potential to get more history books for free! Simply visit the link below to join.

Captivatinghistory.com/ebook

Also, make sure to follow us on Facebook, Twitter and Youtube by searching for Captivating History.

References

[1] Harriet I. Flower, *The Cambridge Companion to the Roman Republic*, Cambridge University Press, 2006

[2] Mary Beard, *SPQR: A History of Ancient Rome*, Profile Books, London, 2015

[3] The word 'candidate' derives from the Latin candidatus, which means 'whitened' and refers to the specially whitened togas that Romans wore during election campaigns, to impress the voters. (Beard)

[4] A letter to Atticus

[5] Titus Livius (59 BC – 17 AD) was a Roman historian. His history of Rome from its foundation to his own time contained 142 books, of which 35 survive.

[6] As referred by Beard (*SPQR, A History of Ancient Rome*)

[7] According to Livy

[8] Publius Ovidius Naso, *The Art of Love (Ars Amatoria)*, Book One, available online at: https://en.wikisource.org/wiki/Ars_Amatoria:_The_Art_of_Love/1

[9] *The Guardian*, "Ovid's exile to the remotest margins of the Roman empire revoked" https://www.theguardian.com/world/2017/dec/16/ovids-exile-to-the-remotest-margins-of-the-roman-empire-revoked

[10] David M. Gwynn, *The Roman Republic: A Very Short Introduction*, Oxford University Press; 2012

[11] Plutarch, *Moralia, On the fortune of the Romans* http://www.gutenberg.org/ebooks/23639

[12] Livy; also: T. P. Wiseman, *Remus: A Roman Myth*. New York: Cambridge University Press, 1995

[13] Painting by Jean Bardin, 1765. https://upload.wikimedia.org/wikipedia/commons/d/d5/Bardin_Tullia.jpg

[14] Beard, as above

[15] Beard

[16] Gwynn, as above

[17] Stephen P. Oakley, "The Early Republic," *The Cambridge Companion to the Roman Republic*, edited by Harriet I. Flower, Cambridge University Press, 2006

[18] Gwynn

[19] Oakley, as above

[20] Livy

[21] The word 'dictator' in ancient Rome had a different meaning than it has in modern world. It was a military title, not a synonym for a 'tyrant.'

[22] Michael Grant, *History of Rome*, Faber, 1979

[23] These were the same walls that were said to have been built by Servius Tullius and are still known as the "Servian Walls"

[24] Alexander the Great's brother-in-law

[25] Polybius was a pro-Roman Greek historian from Megalopolis

[26] Gwynn

[27] Livy

[28] Livy

[29] Gwynn

[30] Plutarch, *Life of Flamininus*

[31] "Greece, the captive, made her savage victor captive, and brought the arts into rustic Latium." Horace, Epistles 2.1.156, in Horace: *Satires, Epistles, and Ars Poetica*

[32] Polybius, Histories

[33] Beard

[34] Cited according to Beard; the exact source unknown

[35] The Cambridge Companion to the Roman Republic Cambridge University Press, 2006

[36] Latin: King.

[37] Octavius's family was from Thurii, hence the addition of the name Thurinus.

[38] Beard (*SPQR, a History of Ancient Rome*) and others: Octavian made a pogrom to get rid of his political opponents, just like Sulla did, but did not want to be remembered like a ruthless one, but rather a revered one, an "Augustus.'

[39] Bust of the emperor with the Civic Crown, Palace Bevilacqua, Verona, Italy / Wikimedia Commons.

[40] A Philippic was a harsh critique in a tradition established by the Greek orator Demosthenes who criticized Philip II of Macedon in the 4th century BC.

[41] Phil. 13.10 "Existimasne igitur, M. Lepide, qualem Pompeium res publica habitura sit ciuem, talis futuros in re publica Antonios? in altero pudor, grauitas, moderatio, integritas; in illis - et cum hos compello, praetereo animo ex grege latrocini neminem - libidines, scelera, ad omne facinus immanis audacia." (Well, Marcus Lepidus, do you think that the res publica will find in Pompeius the kind of citizen which the Antonii will be to the res publica? In him there is modesty, responsibility, even-handedness and honesty; in them (and along with them I cannot help thinking of every one of their robber gang) lusts,

crimes and a monstrous effrontery ready for any circumstance.)

[42] Present-day Bologna.

[43] Plutarch, Life of Antony, The Parallel Lives of the Greeks and Romans, http://penelope.uchicago.edu/Thayer/E/Roman/Texts/Plutarch/Lives/Antony*.html.

[44] Plutarch, as above.

[45] As above

[46] Plutarch, as above.

[47] Gaius Suetonius Tranquillus, De vita Caesarum (The Twelve Caesars), AD 121 (the reign of the emperor Hadrian).

[48] In "The Parallel Lives of the Greeks and Romans," Plutarch uses the name (or title?) Caesar consistently. A number of rulers that followed had names that started with Gaius Julius Caesar. Augustus was Gaius Julius Caesar Augustus; Nero was Gaius Julius Caesar Nero, and so forth.

[49] Publius (or Gaius) Cornelius Tacitus, Annales (The Annals).

[50] A statue of Augustus from the 1st century AD, discovered 1863 in Villa Livia, Prima Porta, Rome / Wikimedia Commons.

[51] The Roman emperor Augustus represented in his role of pontifex maximus, approx. 20 BC, National Museum of Rome / Wikimedia Commons.

[52] Greg Rowe, "The Emergence of Monarchy: 44 BCE–96 CE" in: *A companion to the Roman Empire* by David Potter (editor) / *Blackwell companions to the ancient world*, Blackwell Publishing Ltd, 2006.

[53] As cited in Greg Rowe, "The Emergence of Monarchy: 44 BCE–96 CE" (as above).

[54] Beard, as above

[55] Ovid, *Metamorphoses*, Book VI.

[56] Rowe, as above.

[57] Anthony Barrett, *Caligula: The Abuse of Power*, Routledge, 2015.

[58] Image source: Wikimedia Commons. The complete Julio-Claudian family tree is available here: https://en.wikipedia.org/wiki/Julio-Claudian_family_tree.

[59] Rowe.

[60] Gaius Suetonius Tranquillus, The Twelve Caesars: The Life of Tiberius.

[61] Photo title "Roman Empire: Gaius Caligula. 37-41 AD. Æ Sestertius (26.83 g, 7h). Rome mint. Struck 37-38 AD. C CAESAR AVG GERMANICVS PON M TR POT, laureate head left: AGRIPPINA DRVSILLA IVLIA, S C in exergue, Gaius' three sisters standing facing: Agrippina (as Securitas) leaning on column, holding cornucopiae, and placing hand on Drusilla (as Concordia), holding patera and cornucopiae; Julia (as Fortuna) holding rudder and cornucopiae." CC by Classical Numismatic Group, Inc.

[62] Detail from the painting A Roman Emperor 41 AD by Lawrence Alma-Tadema / Wikipedia Commons

[63] Imperial portrait of Roman emperor (41–54 AD) Claudius (10 BC–54 AD) Source: Wikimedia Commons.

[64] Gaius Suetonius Tranquillus, The Twelve Caesars: The Life of Claudius.

[65] Suetonius, The Lives of Twelve Caesars, Life of Nero and Cassius Dio, Roman History.

[66] Tacitus, Histories.

[67] Portrait of Nero. Marble, Roman artwork, 1st century CE. From the Augustan area on the Palatine Hill. Antiquarium of the Palatine; source: Wikimedia Commons.

[68] Tacitus, Annales.

[69] Tacitus, as above

[70] Suetonius, Cassius Dio, Pliny the Elder.

[71] Image source: (CC) Classical Numismatic Group.

[72] Suetonius, as above

[73] Suetonius, as above.

[74] Image courtesy of Chris Parker via Flickr (CC BY-SA 2.0).

[75] Gaius Suetonius Tranquillus, The Twelve Caesars: The Life of Claudius.

[76] The bust of Titus, the Capitoline museum. CC by Sailko / Wikipedia Commons.

[77] Bust of the Emperor Domitian, Louvre / Wikimedia Commons.

[78] Brian W. Jones, *The Emperor Domitian*, 1993.

[79] Suetonius, as above.

[80] Machiavelli, Discourses on Livy

[81] Machiavelli, as above

[82] Edward Gibbon, "The History of the Decline and Fall of the Roman Empire," 1997 Project Gutenberg Edition http://www.gutenberg.org/files/25717/25717-h/25717-h.htm#latter.

[83] As above.

[84] Cassius Dio, Roman History.

[85] As above.

[86] Michael Peachin, Rome the Superpower: 96–235 CE; in: *A companion to the Roman Empire* by David Potter (editor) / *Blackwell companions to the ancient world*, Blackwell Publishing Ltd, 2006.

[87] Wikimedia Commons

[88] Cassius Dio, as above.

[89] As above.

[90] Bennett, Julian (2001). Trajan. Optimus Princeps. Bloomington: Indiana University Press.

[91] Busts of Hadrianus in Venice / Wikimedia Commons.

[92] Scriptores Historiae Augustae, Hadrian.

[93] Historia Augusta (c. 395) Hadr.

[94] Cassius Dio, as above

[95] Marcus Aurelius, *Meditations*, http://www.gutenberg.org/ebooks/2680.

[96] Marble portrait bust of Marcus Aurelius. Roman, Antonine period, 161-180 AD. Metropolitan Museum of Art, New York / Public Domain Image.

[97] Cassius Dio, as above.

[98] Beard, as above.

[99] Bust of Commodus as Hercules, with the lion skin, the club and the golden apples of the Hesperides. Roman artwork. Palazzo dei Conservatori, Hall of the Horti Lamiani / Wikimedia Commons.

[100] Cassius Dio, as above

[101] Lars Brownworth, *Lost to the West: The Forgotten Byzantine Empire That Rescued Western Civilization*, Crown Publishing, New York, 2009.

[102] Brownworth, as above; Edward Gibbon, *The History Of The Decline And Fall Of The Roman Empire*, Vol. Five, Project Gutenberg edition: http://www.gutenberg.org/files/735/735-h/735-h.htm

[103] Brownworth, as above

[104] Learn more about Augustus and the Principate in Book 2 of *Ancient Rome* - "The Roman Empire"

[105] Timothy E. Gregory, *A History of Byzantium*. Malden, MA: Blackwell Publishing, 2005.

[106] Image courtesy of Katie Chao/MOMA/Wikimedia Commons (CC)

[107] Brownworth, as above

[108] Image courtesy of Jorge Láscar/Flickr (CC) https://www.flickr.com/photos/8721758@N06/10350972756

[109] Brownworth, as above

[110] Gregory, as above

[111] Julian, as cited by Brownworth (see above)

[112] Image courtesy of Classical Numismatic Group/Wikipedia Commons

[113] As cited on https://en.wikipedia.org/wiki/List_of_oracular_statements_from_Delphi ; Five different translations available here: http://laudatortemporisacti.blogspot.com/2012/12/the-last-oracle.html

[114] Gibbon, as above

[115] Image courtesy of Petar Milosevic/Wikipedia Commons

[116] Gregory, as above

[117] "I do not care whether or not it is proper for a woman to give brave counsel to frightened men; but in moments of extreme danger, conscience is the only guide. Every man who is born into the light of day must sooner or later die; and how can an Emperor ever allow himself to become a fugitive? If you, my Lord, wish to save your skin, you will have no difficulty in doing so. We are rich, there is the sea, there too are our ships. But consider first whether, when you reach safety, you will not regret that you did not choose death in preference. As for me, I stand by the ancient saying: royalty makes the best shroud."— Empress Theodora (recorded by Procopius, as cited in Brownsworth)

[118] Image courtesy of Arild Vågen (Wikipedia Commons)

[119] Brownworth, as above

[120] The five Great Christian Seas or the Five Patriarchates were Rome, Constantinople, Jerusalem, Antioch, and Jerusalem, which made the Pentarchy of Christianity.

[121] Gregory, as above

[122] Brownworth, as above

[123] Gregory, as above

[124] Author unknown/public domain

[125] Brownworth, as above

[126] As cited by Brownworth

[127] Gibbon, as above

[128] Norwich, John Julius. Byzantium: The Decline and Fall. New York: Alfred A. Knopf, 2003.

[129] Norwich, as above

[130] Gibbon, as above

Made in the USA
Columbia, SC
11 July 2025